C000145196

to you

Chapter 0:
Instrumental Intro

We've all used something or someone to escape ourselves at one point or another. Maybe it was a Netflix binge and a glass of wine at the end of a stressful workday. Or a partner who we changed our lives for, in hopes that they would make us feel good enough. Or those hours of free time we sacrificed for that job.

The danger, of course, doesn't come from a casual cocktail, one day of working overtime, or scrolling social media for too long on a Saturday. It comes from attaching our identities to external things and never confronting who we are at our core. This attachment has the ability to destroy us, our loved ones, and our community, unless we stop escaping and learn how to take back our power.

For me, that escape has always been alcohol. The annual weekend of total madness in Villach embodied this love affair. Villach is an Austrian city across the border from Italy, where the "Villacher Kirchtag," literally the Villach Church Day, takes place every summer. A better name for the event, coined by my friends and I, is the Austrian Beer Festival.

During my time in the Italian army, I was stationed in Udine. Any escape from the constant drilling and marching of army life was welcome, especially if it involved beer. When a friend told me about Villacher Kirchtag, it made its way to the top of my weekend bucket list.

One Friday in August of 2000, long after I left the military, three friends and I ventured to the infamous Villacher Kirchtag. We left after dinner and arrived there around midnight. But something wasn't right. The streets were barren, without a soul around, much less a pint of beer. Our trip must have been a bust. Where was this famed Villacher Kirchtag?

We drove through the deserted city streets until we came across a riverbank crowded with tents. Next to the riverbank was a glowing city center, full of party lights and drunkenness. The entire old town gathered in the center for beer stands, traditional Austrian food, singing, and dancing. Drunk people were everywhere and it felt like a space where anyone could do anything without being judged–a state of party freedom.

We found a table, the rain pattering against the wooden roof covering it, and a German waiter who looked like a younger, chubbier Freddy Mercury served us Austrian kebabs and beers. The waiter didn't add most of them to our bill, encouraging us to order even more beers. We drank and drank and drank until the beer stands closed. The four of us headed back to our tent, drunk and soaked from the storm.

Rain pounded against our tent for the entire night... or so we thought until a funky smell greeted us the next morning. How had we been able to sleep with such an odor? And what could even make such a stench in the first place? As we got out of the tent, the source revealed itself: piss. We had placed our tent right under a wall where people relieved themselves onto our tent for the entire night.

Despite the unusual rainstorm, I fell in love with the madness of it all. The next year, we returned with three more friends, bringing our group up to seven happy drunks. And we didn't camp out in the same place that time!

For the next ten years, we invited more friends and the memories became louder, crazier, and more obnoxious. After a couple of years, we even started making T-shirts with a motto to express how serious we were: **NO H2O.** Each year, we made the unofficial uniform in a different color, but always in a bright shade so we could find each other in the chaos of the beer festival.

To get a better idea of what a Villach weekend looked like, I created a scorecard. Add up the points based on how many were accomplished in a single night. My score for one night is 3,250 points and my score for all Villach days put together would be 7,100. Free beers to the person with the highest score 🫣

Drinking	Socializing	Dancing	Vomiting	Wandering	Waking up
Drink one beer 50	Buy a round of beers 50	Dance to the music 50	See someone vomit 50	Get lost with friends 50	In a tent alone 50
Drink three beers 100	Play carnival games 100	Dance and sing 100	Vomit alone 100	Get lost alone 100	In a car alone 100
Drink five beers 200	Go on the rides 200	Dance in a group 200	Vomit twice 200	Find new friends 200	On the ground alone 200
Drink ten beers 500	Prank a stranger 500	Dance with a stranger 500	Vomit on someone 500	Enjoy the nightclub 500	With a stranger 500
Drink a crate of beer 1000	Fall asleep in public 1000	Dance on a table 1000	Vomit with someone 1000	Get escorted by the police 1000	At the hospital 1000

A weekend at Villach wasn't truly a Villach Weekend without at least one person passed out in the corner, someone dancing on a table, and someone throwing up on one of the fair rides. And I often completed all three. In fact, my picture at the back of the book was taken on a Saturday morning in 2006 after a night spent unconsciously sleeping in the dirt, and in 2011, I drank so much I forgot my entire stag weekend!

Despite the blurred memories of the event, the feeling of community never faded. Villach was the type of thing we all prioritized. At the beginning of the year, we marked off the weekend on our calendar with the color for that year's T-shirt already selected. No matter what each year brought, I could depend on my Villach friends for a good time.

During one of my most drunk years (2009), I slumped on a bench close to the city center after too many beers. Two girls approached and as they saw me, they sat with me instead of running away (shockingly). I was so drunk, I couldn't see straight, but the girls waited with me. Waited for what–I didn't know. After a while, the police arrived. My heart sank into my chest as I realized the two girls had called the police on me. Images of taking my mug shot drunk flashed across my mind–and it wasn't a pretty picture.

Luckily, the police drove me to the campsite in their car. None of my friends were at the campsite so instead of sleeping, like the police had told me to, I went back to town. By one am, there were pictures of me with my friends again.

When I did find my friends, they asked if I felt my teeth large. (Whenever I drank, my teeth felt larger than life and my friends and I would joke about it. We'll probably hear this phrase in other chapters too.) Instead of answering, I ordered another round of beers.

Insane Drinking Wisdom
WHEN THIRSTY ON A NIGHT OUT,
DRINK ANOTHER BEER, NOT WATER.

Each year, we increased in numbers and fun until we reached a peak about eight years after the first weekend. That year, our group was forty strong–a true brotherhood of beers and adventure. I wondered how the next year could possibly beat it.

And it didn't. Our numbers decreased the next year. And the one after that. And the one after that. Friends canceled as they started families, got promotions, or simply grew out of that stage of their life. I tried to negotiate and get people to keep coming, but the decline couldn't be stopped.

Almost everything in nature follows this cycle of peaks and declines, including the weekend trip to Villach. I had depended on the surety of the weekend and didn't like when that certainty was swept out from under me.

We've all grown apart from a group of friends. Sometimes, we find we have nothing in common with high school friends when we return to our hometown. Or we move for work and find it difficult to Facetime every week. No matter the reason, friendship breakups hurt.

By 2015, the group was almost as small as the first year and we stayed for only a night instead of the whole weekend. That final year didn't have the same upbeat vibe as the others. Seven of us sat around a small table, remembering the magic of past years. We probably should have chosen black instead of green for the T-shirts–the energy was similar to a funeral. Villach was dead ☠️

Our world is in a constant state of trying to avoid the natural decline, like my struggle against Villach ending. Think about the constant economic growth we have been pursuing for the last few decades. The more effort we put into pushing upwards, the harder we will fall after the peak has been reached. We need to feel not only the ups, but also the downs.

We're all consumed with what's around us, including alcohol. Yet, so many of us lean into the fun, ignore the inevitable fall, and keep reaching for higher peaks. This process is poisoning the three levels of influespire–speaking of, let's take a break to explain what they are and how they control our lives.

We don't grow up in a vacuum, but in three levels of influespire. Influespire is a term that refers to how we are both influenced (passive forces) and inspired (active forces) by these three levels, and we act in a certain way based on how much we are either influenced or inspired. Our society, pack, and self influespire us to act and react in different ways.

If the influence and inspiration are positive, we are positively influespired. If either is negative, then we are negatively influespired. While we can sometimes overcome a negative influespire, it is more difficult. Luckily, we can control how we interact with the environment and how we influence others.

For example, someone who sees society as working against them, has friends who spend every night partying, and who has a negative self view would be negatively influespired. When that person stops and recognizes how these forces are impacting their life and decisions, they can decide to take control. They could shift their view of society, change their friends, and work toward self love.

We can also switch how we influespire others as well. Sometimes, one kind word or accomplishing a goal others thought was impossible can shift our influespire over them. It can be a ripple effect to motivate others to go after their dreams–and be a source of positive influespire on others.

When we don't understand these levels, our insecurities are heightened and we are influenced to take the wrong actions. Our power is diminished. But when we take the time to understand them, we can better navigate the world and make our dreams come true. When we can recognize and respond instead of reacting to these levels of influespire, our impact can be limitless.

THREE LEVELS OF INFLUESPIRE

The first level of influespire is **our self**. We are unique. We are all physically different. Not one of us is the same as anyone else. Even "identical" twins are different from one another.

In the second level, we are influespired by **our pack**–those ride or dies who are always there for us. Our family and those close to us are unique and unlike anyone else's pack. Whatever form of intimate reality we have, it's different from the one anyone else has, though it usually consists of the one to 20 people that are closest to us.

Finally, we are influespired by **the society** we grew up in. Each society has its own culture, vices, and virtues. This level is where we often lose ourselves as we believe we are too small to change it.

Throughout my life, I've been fortunate to experience multiple societies. I was born in Italy and spent a year in the United States, my early 30s in the United Kingdom, and most of the rest of my life in the Netherlands. For my job, I frequently traveled for months on end to Brazil, Colombia, South Africa, Poland, Turkey, Russia, and India, among other countries. In total, I've visited 45 countries and lived in four. I don't say this to brag about how well traveled I am or to set this up as a travel book (though I might give some travel tips). Instead, I want to stress that the principles in this book can apply to us all, despite our cultural differences.

My community, the culture I lived in, and even who I was, has changed many times. But one principle stayed the same: life is always changing. It happens in cycles. This universal truth applies to every level of experience and every person alive.

Societies come and go. People build walls and cities, but these structures always come down, from the Great Wall of China to Rome. I will say our societies have grown bigger as smaller ones have died out and joined together. The picture shows how society is evolving, even as some fight against it in the name of nationalism.

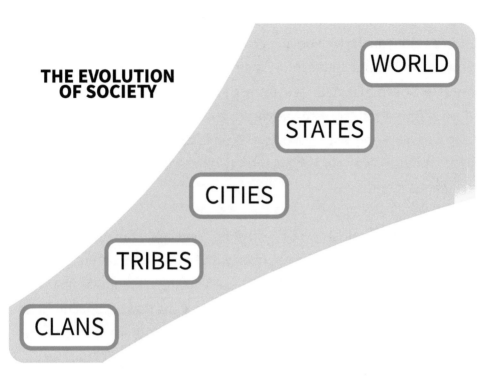

THE EVOLUTION OF SOCIETY

WORLD

STATES

CITIES

TRIBES

CLANS

Our packs come and go. Friends we thought would be at every birthday party move across the country. Partners we wanted to grow old with instead grow distant until one day the relationship ends. A family member decides to estrange themself from the family. While not all friendships and relationships end, they all go through ups and downs. Some of my friendships from my childhood in Italy have lasted to this day, but I sometimes talk to these people every week and at other times, we hardly talk at all.

Even as individuals, we ebb and flow. In some seasons, we are productive, vibrant, and exploring all the world has to offer. At other times, we need to rest, to look introspectively and heal, and to move slower. We are not the same as we were ten years ago and we are not who we will be ten years from now. Even in ten months, ten days, or ten minutes, we could be an entirely different person. Life is change and this is natural.

But we all fight against this cycle in almost every area of our lives. When the cycle is going up, we are ok with how life moves. For example, I had no trouble inviting more people and having more fun at the annual weekend in Villach. But when it was going down, I became such a powerful fighter, I could take on a spartan. Or, more accurately in my case, I could become someone who ended friendships over canceled Villach weekends.

Everyone plans for the peaks and growth. Nobody plans for the downturn. In reality, everything has a cycle. Everything comes in waves, from light to music to our lives. This is inescapable and we all need to learn how to work together for the well-being of the planet and ourselves.

Think of the desperate grabs political leaders make when they're about to lose power, such as how Stalin monitored everyone's actions with secret police in order to maintain power. Even before Stalin, Russia had a long history of leaders who would take any step possible to stay in control.

After the death of Catherine the Great, a beloved Russian leader, her son, Tsar Paul, took over. In comparison to his mother, he was a weak ruler who was criticized by almost everyone at court. But he also had dreamed of power his entire life and when he was crowned Tsar at the age of 42, he wasn't about to let the critics take it away.

One of his favorite tactics was to exile anyone who didn't agree with him to Siberia. When someone was exiled in tsarist Russia, they couldn't go home and collect their belongings or get any money from the bank. They were directly loaded into a cart and transported to the cold, outer province of the empire. So many people were exiled to Siberia during Paul's reign, it was common to wear winter coats full of rubles around court, even in the heat of summer, just in case the Tsar decided to exile them.

Ultimately, he lost power four years after his coronation. Everyone in the country, including his son, grew tired of his antics and the nobles decided to assassinate him. Some historians believe his son was involved. When a coup run by the ruler's son leads to someone's demise, he must have been a bad apple.

Businesses around the world have a plan for how they will triple revenue next year, but very few I've consulted with have a plan for seasons where business is slow and profits decrease. Even when businesses have almost a complete monopoly, they'll attack the only competitors left instead of accepting that they won't keep growing naturally.

The internet is one of the spaces where we see what a company with a monopoly will do to stay in power. Meta, the owner of Facebook and Instagram, controls much of the social media space while Google, Amazon, and Apple have monopolies over their respective fields. In some countries, Facebook is the only access point the majority of people have to the internet. The word Facebook is synonymous with the internet in the Philippines because most people's phones only connect to Facebook and they can't access other websites. But even with this near monopoly, Meta devotes thousands of dollars each year to trying to put TikTok, one of their biggest competitors, out of business.

By consolidating power instead of allowing for healthy competition (i.e. focusing on better serving customers instead of companies undermining their competitors), companies fight against the natural rise and decline. They create a false illusion that their business will be in a state of constant growth, but the lack of planning for the inevitable declines will only hurt workers and clients.

As individuals, we fight against endings too. We've all known someone who refused to stop drunk calling an ex or who refused to let their kids make their own decisions when choosing their careers. And surely we can all think of an older family member, especially a grandparent, who doesn't want to give up control of the family, even as their memory wanes.

We can probably also think of times when we fought against the winds of change–when we stayed in that toxic relationship a bit too long or complained about our job instead of brushing up our resume.

WHAT ARE SOME COMMON AREAS IN LIFE WHERE WE RESIST PAIN? WHAT HAPPENS WHEN WE RESIST VS EMBRACE IT?

We fight so hard against the downwind when it would be much easier to let go. Letting go looks like phasing ourselves out of jobs that no longer serve us and searching for new opportunities or changing how often we talk to a family member or friend who has started to drain our energy. In all these situations, we should embrace change and move with it instead of against it. But that's easier said than done.

Part of why we don't let go faster is due to the wrong type of validation from the three levels of influespire, which we will discuss more in the next chapters. For now, I just want to mention one external factor. The source of so many fun–and painful–memories in my life. **Alcohol**.

Call me a retired professional alcoholic. While wine was a big part of my Italian upbringing, I didn't fall into the habit of binge drinking until I traveled to the United States. Later, while in the United Kingdom, I fell into their cultural habit of getting drunk at the local pub each weekend. In every new society after my time in the US and UK, drinking became something which bonded me to others. It was a familiar in the unfamiliar, an escape from any discomfort, and a source of external happiness I craved.

That is until I went through the process I'll explain in this book.
This process allowed me to break my drinking habit and rediscover who
I was. Afterward, I could control what influences I was letting into my life
and I had the tools to build more meaningful connections with those
around me. Even if drinking doesn't affect someone in the same way it
does me, all of us have some source of unhealthy enjoyment, whether
Netflix binging, social media scrolling, smoking, coffee drinking,
or indulging in too many treats.

Today, we have the opportunity to analyze these unhealthy indulgences,
ourselves, and the world around us. We can examine:

- What influences we're letting in
- How we can overcome addictions which numb us
- Who we want to be
- What working with life's cycles instead of against them looks like
- How to shape the communities around us so they foster
  collaboration, not a divide

We have the unique chance to learn how to belong to ourselves instead
of fitting in with a religious, nationalist, or economic scheme.

That's what this book is all about. This book is our guide to confronting
our obsessions and where we might be lying to ourselves. While the
primary focus is on my relationship with alcohol, this love affair is only a
guiding theme–a guide to what happens when we give up our power
and the tools we can use to take our power back 💪

Today we have an opportunity to look at external forces which control us, such as religion, nationalism, and alcohol. Throughout these chapters, we'll be looking at what is good about each of these aspects and which parts of them we can leave behind on our quest to find ourselves and build better communities.

By the end of the book, we'll all be ready to tackle the alcohol in our lives and confront who we really are. By shedding the negative influences and breaking the chains of what numbs us, we'll feel more content in our own lives, packs, and societies AND we'll be armed with the tools needed to save others. Pour a drink and let's get to work healing ourselves and our communities.

Chapter 1:
Alcohol He Knows Me

My love affair with alcohol started at the age of six when my family would give me small sips of wine at dinner. By the age of fourteen, I had a drinking catchphrase. And yes–we could probably call that a drinking problem.

The night my drinking catchphrase was born started with a feeling many of us can relate to: the anxiety over attending my first boy-girl party. My friend group, all guys, had been invited to a party hosted by a girl in our class. And we weren't just any normal group of guy friends. Our group was called club degli sfigati (club of the uncool). Only boys who never had a girlfriend could be part of it. The goal of every member of the club was to leave the club 😄

Obviously, a boy/girl party invite was a big deal to club degli sfigati. And not only would girls be there, the host's parents were out of town. To a fourteen year old boy, there's nothing more exciting–or scary–than being around girls at a parentless party.

The club began drinking before we headed over to the party. Nothing like a bit of liquid luck to make teenage boys act stupider. More of my life has started with liquid luck than I'd care to admit. In fact, this event was where I came up with one of my first drinking wisdoms that kept me justifying all the drunken nonsense.

Insane Drinking Wisdom
IF WE'RE NERVOUS ABOUT AN EVENT, DRINK UNTIL THE ANXIETY HAS RESIDED... OR UNTIL WE PASS OUT. EITHER MAKES THE SITUATION MORE BEARABLE.

By the time we got to the girl's house, the world tilted from the wine, but I still wanted more. After dinner, we combined Italian gelato with Vodka and the rest of the night wooshed by in a blur. Anytime I talked to someone, either my words or my body swayed, making it impossible for me to hold a conversation without feeling like a drunken sailor. I found myself sitting outside in the cold, too drunk to care that I was shivering. When I went inside, it wasn't because of my friends begging me to come in, but to throw up.

As I barged into the bathroom, vomit rose up and the toilet sat too far away. I puked in the sink and a sensation which would become a constant in my life (until I gave up drinking at 42 years-old) came up. My teeth felt large, the spaces between them bigger. The vomit and the alcohol consumed my mouth, which could not hold anything back. My teeth were the only thing I could feel in my body.

I puked and puked until there was nothing in my stomach left to hurl up. Then, I dry heaved. Breath heavy and the taste of vomit on my tongue, my teeth felt larger than any other body part. When I came out of the bathroom, a friend asked, "Aureo, feeling alright?" I slapped him on the back and flashed a smile, careful not to show my teeth. "I'm fine, except I feel my teeth large."

My friend barked out laughter and guided me back to the group. The sensation of fitting in–of being relatable to others–warmed me. Each time I got drunk after that night, I told people the same thing. **I feel my teeth large.** By the time I turned 20, friends and acquaintances considered "I feel my teeth large," a way to describe drunks, to be my catchphrase. And we all remember the phrase from Villach in the previous chapter.

I not only found my catchphrase in Vittorio Veneto, but had many of my formative moments there. They say we never forget our first love, but our first home is just as memorable, especially when it provides a favorite vice, like Vittorio Veneto gave me. As the name says, my hometown is in Veneto and, more precisely, near the UNESCO world heritage site Le Colline del Prosecco di Conegliano Veneto.

The region has two main exports: alcohol and religion. Most of the world's prosecco and nine popes come from Veneto.

It is not hard to imagine what type of society I was raised in. Wine was everywhere all the time; no one could escape it. I have had regular tastes of wine since I was six years old. During my primary school years, a normal lunch included wine in a glass with water and sugar; most times, instead of drinking it, I would drench bread in the mixture and eat it. I know, it's revolting 🤢

Anyways, wine was always on the table and, as a kid, I would be offered a small sip every now and then, for no apparent reason. To think that today I don't even give Coca-Cola to my children, because of its adverse health effects. It makes me wonder what people around me believed back then. Throughout my teenage years, wine flowed regularly and I always had access to it. That is, until I was seventeen and traveled to a land with a teenage prohibition, but we will get to that story in the next chapter.

The other export of Veneto, religion, made my teeth large in an entirely different way. My family lived in the main square of Ceneda, a neighborhood in Vittorio Veneto, right across the street from the cathedral. Two nuns were part of my family and my grandad worked as a secretary at the Seminario, where men from all over the world came for religious training to enter the priesthood. Every Sunday, we'd attend a packed church service. In the 80s, every mass was full of eager church-goers. The bishop lived in a castle on a hill, overlooking the city.

Basically, Catholicism was impossible to escape. Even in school, religion played a role. The cross reigned above all students and the priest substituted the teacher for one hour each week. Theoretically, we were allowed to opt out, but the very few who did were choosing to live as outcasts. On top of the school's sessions, every child in town also went to Sunday School. Talk about brainwashing an entire generation. Let's take a step back and look at why religions brainwash us.

Religion comes in different shapes and forms, influencing the second and third levels of influespire, and every one of us interprets it the way we want. It grows out of people's beliefs and these beliefs affect the way religion is enforced on other people. Religion is so powerful that today, it influences, and in some cases controls, governments and consequently our lives, whether we believe in religion or not.

Self Discovery Exercise
WHAT COMES TO MIND WHEN SOMEONE SAYS *THE WORD RELIGION?*
WHAT MEMORIES, IDEAS, AND CONCEPTS ARE RELATED TO THAT *DEFINITION OF RELIGION?*

The answer to this prompt will differ for all of us. We've all had very different religious experiences and these have impacted not only our relationship to religion, but to our pack, those from different cultures, and ourselves.

Someone who was raised in a loving religious organization which was accepting and collaborative with different religions might have a more positive view than someone who was raised in an oppressive religious setting with strict rules and harsh punishments. The second group is also more likely to have lower self-esteem, as they look to a god outside themselves for approval, and might be distrusting or judgmental of those around them. But I'm getting ahead of myself. Let's start with the root of all religion: belief.

Belief is the key to understanding religion, because without it, any religion becomes meaningless and useless. As a matter of fact, many religions disappeared in the past because people stopped believing in them. No forgotten god came to hunt down people who stopped believing in them. Conversely, other new religions have appeared because people started believing in them.

When we believe in a religion, leader, or organization we give power to it. Without belief, a religion would lose all its power.

So obviously belief is important to religious leaders. In many ways, it's more important than money. That's why these leaders promise us what we want most–and that we can obtain that thing if we follow them since we can't find it in ourselves... or so they want us to believe.

The most common promise sold in exchange for belief is that of an afterlife. Present in most religions, an afterlife is the promise of immortality. Even the hope of immortality is sufficient for many people to devote their entire life to a religion. No one wants to die–or believe their loved ones can die–so of course we will pledge allegiance to a religion which promises us eternal life. To achieve the reward, we just need to do everything a religion preaches. Easy, right?

Religion is often codified to give a meaning to people's lives and to explain the unknown and metaphysical reality. But in reality, it is used to control and subjugate people. And boy, do many religions have a lot of rules for us to follow. Most major world religions set up complex rules and rituals for followers, such as praying five times a day or donating at least 10% of everything one makes to the church. Don't eat meat, except for fish on Fridays, during lent for Catholics. Hindus shouldn't eat meat at all. Buddhists better meditate daily while Jews need to buy kosher foods during religious holidays. It can be a lot. And much of it doesn't make sense or support the main purpose of each (and all) religion. While each religion has a very different set of rules, the main idea behind every religion is the same: love thy neighbor 😇

Don't believe me? Check out key passages from five of the major religious texts about the importance of love:

Thou shall not take vengeance or bear a grudge against members of thy people. Love thy fellow [Israelite] as thyself.

◉ Leviticus 19:18 (the Torah)

Serve Allah and ascribe no partner to Him. Do good to thy parents, to near of kin, to orphans, and to the needy, and to the neighbor who is of kin and to the neighbor who is a stranger, and to the companion by thy side, and to the wayfarer, and to those whom thy right hands possess.

◉ Quran 4:36

O Ashwin Kumar!
We, lovers, walk together
Live together
Move forward together
With the feeling of togetherness
With the togetherness of hearts

◉ Atharvaveda 2/30/3

Little though he recites the sacred texts, but puts the Teaching into practice, forsaking lust, hatred, and delusion, with true wisdom and emancipated mind, clinging to nothing of this or any other world–he indeed partakes of the blessings of a holy life.

◉ Dhammapada, verse 20

If anyone says, "I love God," and hates his brother, he is a liar; for he who does not love his brother whom he has seen cannot love God whom he has not seen. And this commandment we have from him: whoever loves God must also love his brother.

○ 1 John 4:20-21 (the Bible)

Every religion intends to help us love others and build communities… in theory. In reality, they set up rules that make us different from those around us. They go to war with other religions… even though most religious texts convey the same message of love and community. Sometimes, they even argue over who is better at the same religion (hello Catholics vs Protestants during the Reformation).

Instead of praying for the weak, religions prey on the weak.

When we think about it, we quickly realize that religion is nothing more than comfort food. A nice warm blanket that protects us from our fears. Religion, alcohol, and so many of the other ways we numb ourselves come from society, this third level of influespire. Societal factors influence us in similar ways and can include (but are not limited to):

- Religion
- Alcohol
- Sugar
- Fast food
- Nationalism
- Drugs
- Smoking
- Exercise or dieting
- Comparison, especially on social media
- Escaping into stories, whether through movies, TV shows, or books
- Power over others

In moderation, these are good. There's nothing wrong with enjoying an ice cream or attending mass. The danger comes from when these things consume us–aka when we feel like we depend on them for validation and can't live without them. Sadly, this is becoming more and more common in the modern world.

In 2019, I traveled for work to Dubrovnik, another UNESCO World Heritage Site. While there, I took the opportunity to visit, among other things, the Imperial Fortress at the top of Sdr Hill. The fort today hosts the exhibition about the Homeland War of 1991-1995. It is an incredible display of the atrocities that took place during the Croatian War of Independence, in particular the siege of Dubrovnik. This was an opportunity to learn about a war that, different from many others, took place so close to home and within my lifetime.

But the city contained tourists, unbothered if they stepped on something historical and not understanding the impact of the space. They shouted, "Is this where Cersei took her last stand?" and "where was Jon Snow in that one scene?" Fans of Game of Thrones had conquered Dubrovnik; they were impossible to escape. The vast majority of tourists were missing a chance to learn about real human wickedness and suffering, opting for a selfie at a place where something that does not exist did not happen 🙄

Instead of respecting a place where an army shot human rights in the heart within our lifetimes, the tourists around me came to see where Game of Thrones was shot on camera. Given the number of "believers" it might be possible for Jon Snow, with his dubious birth and resurrection, to become a new Jesus Christ at the center of a new religion.

These new, potent forms of religion have started to take over our society. Television obsessions, infatuation with celebrities, and blindly following political leaders are new ways for the third level of influespire to convince us to look outside ourselves for validation. While it's easier than ever to fall into fanaticism today, it's also easier to find ourselves. For much of history, people didn't have the time to stop and examine these levels of influespire. They couldn't see the differences, influences, and changes needed in all three levels.

Despite my caution about becoming dependent on religion (or religion look-alikes), there is one thing from my religious upbringing which always resonated with me: communion. Many Christians now see it as a mere function without appreciating its true meaning. Today, communion means that we go to the altar, take a piece of dried bread in our mouth, go back and stand in silence, thinking about connecting with the Lord. How is that communion? Communion should be achieved by interacting and engaging with one another, not through solo contemplation. I mean, does no one else find this a bit weird?

We can only be in true communion with others when we are in communion with our own power and when we feel like we belong to a group. Religion states our power comes from outside of us–in the form of a god who puts power in us. And here lies the biggest sin of religion: teaching people that god is someone else. Many religions, like Catholicism, still believe god is in every one of us, but it is someone else in us, not us.

We are God! All of us together, in true communion, become God.

Whenever we collaborate, we accomplish more than if we act on our own. Think about two of us having to move two tables from one house to another. If we took one table each, it would be much harder than if we cooperate and move both tables together.

So many of us are moving tables alone, unaware of the divides in our society and how much stronger we are lifting a table together. Some are even moving entire kitchens by themselves. We still pursue theories that divide us, such as religion, rather than those that unite us. We pursue things outside ourselves and feel a need to prove ourselves instead of leaning into the truth of who we are.

We are GODs: Generators of Dreams

We come up with dreams and, working together, we achieve them. We have been doing this since the dawn of mankind. We dreamt of fire and we made fire. We dreamt of flying and we are flying. We dreamt of the moon and we went to the moon.

This constant dreaming and the relentless pursuit of the best dreams allows us to improve day by day. Our dreams keep us alive, whether we pursue them or not. We can invest our energy in validating ourselves and building community around our dreams, or we can just keep on dreaming and pull our comfort blankets over our eyes as we numb ourselves with society's distractions.

Dreams are like a new favorite jacket. When we buy it at the store, we're so excited about the new piece to add to our collection.
We imagine what everyone will say when they see our awesome new jacket and how much more confident we'll be in it. Then we get home and the fear overtakes us. This new jacket was expensive, after all, and what happens if someone spills coffee on it? Or if it gets a snag and frays? To protect it from the outside world, we sometimes let a new, expensive piece of clothing sit in our drawers, collecting dust.
Yet, like that new jacket, no one else knows our dreams exist unless we wear them proudly. We either flaunt dreams on the streets or let them decay in the drawer.

Take Schrödinger's cat. The cat is or isn't in the box simultaneously (I'm not willing to use the dead-or-alive scenario) until one of us opens the box and checks if the cat is there. Was the cat in the box all along? Or was she never there? By opening the box, we give the cat a chance to exist. But by not opening the box, we condemn the cat to a limbo of non-existence within our reality.

By choosing to act, we give our dreams a much higher probability of realization. Through our efforts, we create reality. And the more we cooperate and work together, the more we can reconcile our realities and breathe life into our biggest dreams. Because we can for sure make small dreams come true on our own, but the more we are and the more we cooperate, the bigger the dreams we can turn into reality.

For example, we dreamt about flying for millennia. And for millennia it remained a dream. A dream so far-fetched that no one seriously believed it was possible. Myths were created around this dream as it was so inconceivable that only gods could achieve it. If a human achieved it, they would be like Icarus, flying too close to the sun and falling. But for so long we forgot that we are GODs, not humans. And ultimately GODs did achieve it. First, through the dreams of GODs such as Leonardo da Vinci who dreamt about it publicly. In the 1700s, the Montgolfier brothers made the dream reality, and the Wright brothers mechanized the dream in the early 1900s.

Religion is a good example of how society influespires us to give up on dreams. Views different from the dogma and doctrine that altered the status quo were heavily contrasted to the point that the people were not willing to pursue their dreams in fear of harm being done to them. Not only that, but many people have steamrolled over others in the name of religion. Countless Popes have started wars, deposed leaders, and impoverished the masses to maintain power. The struggle for power was seen at every stage of a pope's reign, especially in the medieval ages and the renaissance.

One of the most infamous examples was Pope Alexander VI who was pope from 1492-1503. Alexander VI came from the wealthy, corrupt, and infamous Borgia family. In order to get into power, he bought votes from powerful Italian cardinals. Once in power, rumors circled about the many sins of his family, including incest, poison, and money laundering. Pope Alexander VI did everything he could to maintain power, including starting a war against Naples. During the war, he switched sides constantly between his home country of Spain and France. Of course, his allegiance relied on whoever would give more power and arms to keep him in power. His reign ended with many of his political enemies in jail and the Vatican in a state of disarray. He fought against the natural downward cycle of power to maintain his own influespire in the world, not caring about the damage to the Catholic church's image.

And Pope Alexander VI is not the only person to use religious justification to take more power. Leaders across all religions and regions who want to keep power often use religion as a reason for fighting against the downward cycles at the expense of weaker members of society. This still happens today. We still give up our power to external factors–and thus, we forfeit our ability to truly belong to ourselves and in community with those around us.

While religion is the first feature we talk about in the society influespire level, there are also others. The point with any of these societal forces is to analyze how they have control over us and how they make us forget that we are GODs. Religion makes us forget we are GODs by putting our power into a being outside of ourselves, whether a god or a religious figure. Two other common societal forces which threaten our power are nationalism and racism. With both, we are seen as separate from those around us and with nationalism specifically, we look to one political leader or organization for guidance.

Those who manipulate society, whether for political or religious reasons, tell us to look outside of our souls and to see ourselves as separate from those around us. This divides us so we can't work together to accomplish our dreams and tears apart our confidence in our ability to be GODs. When religion or other societal forces take over, we start to actively thwart others' dreams and fight instead of work together. It's time to take back that power.

Self Discovery Exercise
BRAINSTORM A COUPLE OF WAYS WE CAN TAKE BACK OUR POWER FROM RELIGION AND OTHER FALSE COMFORTS.

But enough about religion. Let's go back to the equally inebriating topic at hand: alcohol. While alcohol will be our guiding theme, I invite us to bring our own addictions and skeletons along for the ride. Keep these factors in mind and feel free to apply any of the book's lessons to their influence over the world around us. Next stop: getting drunk in the USA.

Chapter 2:
American Rye

First day of school jitters are bad enough, try doing it in a new country. At the age of seventeen, I found myself at a new school in the United States, the promised land of the 20th century. The town the study abroad program placed me in wasn't the beautiful sandy beaches and mountains I'd expected and the people were not as sexy and perfect as the stereotypes I saw on American TV.

But this was the most powerful nation on Earth. There had to be some secret to happiness, wealth, and beauty that I could discover. Surely school would hit me over the head with all the knowledge I needed to be successful.

As the bell rang, signaling the start of the first period, I was ready to learn all the secrets of this fabled country. But instead of starting the lecture, the teacher faced the flag with stripes and fifty stars hanging in the corner of the classroom. All the students stood up too and turned to face the flag, hands over their chests. Without blinking, they repeated in unison, "I pledge allegiance to the flag of the United States of America…"

I glanced around for some sort of explanation, but no one provided any. Some people glared at me for not standing up, but most were too entranced by their prayer to the American flag. Had I accidentally ended up in a zombie movie instead of the country I'd idolized for so many years?

When I decided to study abroad in the United States, I had expected the glamorous life I saw on 90210, not this. I had fallen for one of America's greatest exports–and everyone else around me had too. America's biggest moneymaker abroad is propaganda, aka the American Dream. It's synonymous with a life where anything is possible if one puts in the work–a fairytale that arguably never existed and could exist in any country (I know this is a contradiction, but it makes sense when we think about it).

Even before I entered the US, I had fallen head over heels for this fantasy. TV brainwashed me into thinking the sunny beaches and glitz of Beverly Hills were the norm in the United States. Here, I could discover my dreams, achieve them, AND look as handsome as a Hollywood star in the process. Or so I thought. The reality didn't match the dream.

Turns out, not everyone in America lives like fictional characters on a scripted TV show. My host family didn't live near the beach, they weren't wealthy beyond what I could imagine, and they acted like humans, not TV show characters.

Before applying I thought, even if I wasn't placed in California, I'd be placed somewhere with mountains, like Colorado or Oregon. Instead they sent me to a place full of cornfields, farmland, and flat plains, aka rural Ohio. I had been placed in Alvada, Ohio, pop. 970. Google it now and look.

Yeah. Not exactly Beverly Hills.

New Riegel, the town near Alvada where I attended school, was a catch-all town for nearby farmers in the middle of nowhere Ohio. The nearest city, Toledo, was over an hour away. Most people in the town grew up and stayed there, with only a few escaping and going to college. Almost everyone there was not only white, but had German ancestry. Anyone who didn't have German-American ancestry was an anomaly. Heck, anyone who wasn't from there was a black sheep. Many citizens lived in trailers. Their lives revolved around Friday night football games and they were in love with the American dream, despite few in town experiencing it.

I was no stranger to nationalism when I arrived. Italy is a country with a lot of nationalism–it's on the inside and not necessarily reflected in the stereotype of the land of pizza and pasta. On the outside, it's seen as a country which would betray its allies, as it did in World War II (even though betraying Germany was the right thing to do).

But that outward betrayal is simply a product of the right and the left fighting internally. Both sides have strong, nationalistic ideas about how Italy should be run.

For years, Italian governments have been strained by this internal division. Leadership changed so quickly that the late Queen of England saw 66 Italian Prime ministers. The current Italian government is even more outwardly nationalistic, with calls for Italy to "Brexit" the EU just a couple of years back. (Today only a fool would propose to follow the UK's footsteps.)

With all that said, Italy's nationalism doesn't even come close to the United States'. Don't get me wrong–there's nothing wrong with loving one's country. In small doses, patriotism is a good quality that can bond fellow citizens, and patriotism has gotten America far as a country. The issue comes when one's pride in their country is at the expense of people outside that country or marginalized communities within the same country.

In the United States, this happens far too often as civil rights battles are fought within and many Americans believe themselves to be "better off" than the rest of the world. Some of the weirdest displays of nationalism I saw in the United States included:

- When I graduated, they gave me a flag as a present as an exchange student. The flag was gifted to me, folded in a specific way and meant to be flown that way–I used it as a curtain.

- The knowledge most Americans I encountered had of Italy when I was there came from the Rocky movie series and the Godfather. References to the Italian Stallion, a horse head in the bed, and the Italian mafia were constant.
- Almost no one in New Reigel followed the World Cup–the most important event in Europe and Latin America. In the US, people are obsessed with sports, but only national ones.

Ok but enough about my time in the US. Let's discuss how a country becomes nationalist, a byproduct of toxic love. There are two main indicators of nationalism:

1. Loving one's country at the expense of others
2. Forcing others to love the country too, even if against their will

For the majority of the 20th century, Americans were drowning in nationalism. They thought they were living in the best country in the world (which is a valid belief if that's what they've been told their entire life and they never had the opportunity to travel elsewhere). The US is one of the countries with the least number of passports, meaning people don't travel abroad and know what life is like outside their country.

In 1994, only 10% of Americans had passports. Today, over 40% of Americans have passports, with people under 30 making up most of the new passport holders. This is still lower than other countries, such as the UK, where 72% of citizens have a passport. With the rise of passport holders and imported culture into the US (hello BTS), there's been more attacks on US nationalism.

Some young Americans now joke that the American dream is to leave their country, though the majority of Americans still view such statements as disrespectful. Even among younger generations in rural areas like Alvada, nationalism is most likely alive and well today. But none of this existed when I lived there in 1994. In the 1990s, there was less skepticism about America's power. After all, the Berlin Wall had just fallen, thanks to **American democracy.**

Of course, the United States isn't the only country with a penchant for nationalism. The world seems to become more nationalistic with each passing decade. To understand why people have such an affinity for where they live, let's look at where these feelings started–with the invention of the nation-state after the medieval ages.

Historians have found something interesting about the so-called dark ages: the medieval ages might not have been as horrible as we think! While the medieval period did have plagues, torture chambers, and other not-so-nice features, it also had open borders, more trade between different ethnic groups, and a fairer distribution of wealth than the centuries after. Yet, because of the power grab of nation-states in the 13th and 14th century, the history was rewritten to make the medieval period the "dark" ages. In contrast, the renaissance, the time of the mighty Spanish and French empires, became an era of light and hope.

History has been rewritten to justify bigger empires, stricter borders, and discrimination against ethnic groups. Now, we live in a world which has shamed the medieval way of thinking. We're told that society is always progressing thanks to the leadership of those in charge instead of recognizing that every time period has both good and bad aspects. Similarly, nations have good and bad aspects, but we're taught to focus on one or the other for each country.

If we continue on the path of nationalism, these nation-state leaders promise things will only keep getting better–even though many of us have found the opposite to be true since the 21st century. This is very similar to how we discussed humankind's fear of the downward trend in the cyclical nature of life, but in the societal influespire.

HISTORICAL PROGRESS

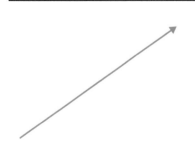 

HOW IT'S COMMONLY TAUGHT | **WHAT IT ACTUALLY LOOKS LIKE**

WHAT IS ONE TIME IN THE HISTORY OF NATIONS OR OUR PERSONAL LIVES WHERE PROGRESS WASN'T LINEAR?
WHAT CAN WE LEARN FROM THAT EVENT?

One of the most famous examples of nationalism is one anyone could guess. In fact, guess which example I'm thinking of right now.

Drumroll please... Nazi Germany is the correct answer. In the mid-20th century, Germany demonstrated how dangerous nationalism could be when they mobilized against the rest of Europe, persecuted Jewish folks and other minorities, and attempted to create one perfect race.

In Man's Search for Meaning, holocaust survivor Viktor Frankl reflected on some truths of surviving nationalism. The main thing that kept prisoners going throughout the Holocaust was the belief it was going to end and there would be something better after. If they stopped believing in a better future, their bodies would give up on them.

While the Nazis are the most extreme example of nationalistic beliefs going too far, many countries are now on a similar track. We are all different, yet nationalism tells us we're all similar... if we are born in the same country. Often, this is done by otherizing different nations or marginalized groups in our own nation (the latter we'll talk more about in the next chapter!). Those who create this fake unity within a country no longer want us to see ourselves as GODs (generators of dreams), but as one collective working toward the leader's dreams.

But back to America, the land of rock and roll, Hollywood, and an unprecedented number of school shootings. My year studying in the United States wasn't the dream I'd imagined. The exchange student who was sent to the same home the year before left within a week. And I understand why. Life in Alvada was boring and the environment was not very foreigner-friendly.

As a single mom to eight children, the host mom assigned to that student and myself had her hands full. Three children, ranging from primary school to senior year of high school, were still living at home as well as an older, adult child who lived there with her husband. The family didn't have enough space for everyone and money was scarce, though dog shit was in ample supply since the family dog defecated inside the house. At least he was regular.

Despite the chaos of this home and lack of resources, my host mom and her family always made me feel welcomed and loved. I stayed for a year and I go back and forth about if that's something to brag about. But the lessons from that period shaped my entire life. In fact, I learned the most influential theme in my life there: **there are no negative experiences. We can get something good out of any experience if we're looking at it the right way.**

I now hold the belief that everyone should be required to live in a different country for six months (minimum!) because of how it can shift our perspective. It doesn't have to be a country with a polar opposite culture. Even my time in Villach, Austria introduced me to a new way of living, despite the fact that Austria is right next door to Italy.

Of course, America was even more of a transformational experience. Since the internet wasn't widespread then, I had few options to communicate back home. I could write letters (and wait two weeks for a response) or I could talk to my family on the home phone. To avoid exchange students becoming too homesick, the study abroad program had a rule that we should only make one call home a month. Given the high intercontinental call fees, it was relatively easy to follow this rule. This lack of connection to Italy enabled me to better immerse myself in the culture. At times, this felt isolating, but it made the experience even more powerful.

If any readers have the chance to go abroad in the modern era, they should try to limit communication with their home country as much as possible.

Along with the lack of mountains, beaches, and gorgeous, thin movie stars, another thing which shocked me about that US town was my education there. Keep in mind I studied abroad in the 1990s in a rural small town–which probably doesn't represent the US education system as a whole. My education in rural America was worse than in Italy, even though the US was the most powerful nation in the world in 1993.

The US had just won the Cold War a couple of years earlier and was setting the agenda for the entire world, yet many Americans weren't even taught where the Berlin Wall was on a map.

In the United States, some are given a good education. Others receive the bare minimum and brainwashing. The brainwashing started in the first period with the pledge of allegiance. During those first weeks in America, I didn't stand up for the pledge. I'd shift uncomfortably under the disapproving stares of my classmates. Part of me wanted to stand up, even though the pledge was one of the least logical things I'd ever seen. I mean, the god they pray to is not even a religious one, but the country itself.

After the pledge one day in October, one of my classmates leaned over and whispered in my ear, "Remember, we can bomb Italy whenever we want."

While not everyone in New Riegel was like this, many reminded me of the power the US held over the rest of the world. Over time, that power compelled me too. The pressure of those around me–the stares which reminded me how different I was–became unbearable. One day I stood up and let nationalism wash over me. I chanted, "I pledge allegiance to the flag..."

As I said the words, I could feel the classroom softening. Fewer eyes glared. The teacher's shoulders relaxed, a small, satisfied smile on his face. I had given up a part of myself to appease the group and the sacrifice had comforted those around me. It had even brought me comfort, but in the way an unhealthy meal does before the heaviness upsets my stomach and I regret the decision.

The brainwashing continued after the last period on Friday, when students would engage in a different type of indoctrination. Fitting in was one of the main lessons taught to American teenagers, both in and outside of school. Teenagers in that small Ohio town would do anything to fit in, from pledging some flag to dressing like everyone else. And when I say they would do anything, I mean anything even if it was forbidden. **Especially if it was forbidden.**

One of the most forbidden activities was drinking. In the United States, people can't drink until the age of 21. Americans can buy a gun at 18, but I couldn't order a glass of wine at prom dinner at that same age. Even if forbidden, every single one of my classmates looked forward to drinking every weekend. On Monday mornings (after the pledge, of course), my fellow students' thoughts shifted to the house party happening on Friday night and those thoughts lasted until they were blackout drunk at the party. By winter, my thoughts constantly wandered to Friday night parties too.

Insane Drinking Wisdom
THERE'S ALWAYS ONE ACTIVITY TO DO ANYWHERE WE TRAVEL TO—AND IT'S A GOOD ONE. WE CAN DRINK UNTIL THE ROOM SPINS!

In earlier chapters we discussed how external sources can influespire us and close us off to our internal guidance. Often, what we are most attracted to is the appeal of what we cannot have: drugs, alcohol, driving a car before getting a license. Even the girls or guys who play hard to get are the most desirable romantic partners. These forbidden activities affect all different levels of influence from the individual to entire nations.

On a societal scale, one of the best examples is the 1920s prohibition in the United States. Before 1920, alcohol was one of the biggest societal problems in the US. Many men who drank gambled away their family's money, cheated on their wives, and hit their children. To combat this, women petitioned for all alcohol to be banned and got their wish on January 17th, 1920.

But the ban wasn't the end of the story. Much of the appeal of the 1920s, even to this day, were the speakeasies. 1920s Americans would flock to these secret clubs and get drunker than ever before. Crime organized around the illegal trade of alcohol, with men like Al Capone making fortunes during this era.

Ironically, when prohibition was lifted in the 1930s, Al Capone and many others like him lost large parts of their fortune as people drank less. Alcohol became an option, not a forbidden vice. Except for teenagers, of course 🙌

In fact, many teenagers in the United States believed a night was wasted unless it ended with blacking out. **Drinking to forget was the goal, even if the pretense is drinking socially.**

Every weekend in New Riegel had the same routine, though the details are blurred, thanks to how much I drank. After school on Friday, we would go over what the weekend plans were: who was hosting the party on Friday? On Saturday during the day? On Saturday night?

I quickly fell into the warm, comforting routine of drinking every weekend. It was one of the times where I got to know my American classmates the best, even if I can't remember all the details from most of the house parties. Underneath the friendliness of these parties, there was a quiet resignation. A resignation that this was all life would be and this was the best way to bond with those around us.

One house party in particular removed the glamor of this illusionary lifestyle. At this party, I realized no one cared if I was there or not. And it wasn't just me. No one there cared who else was there. They only cared about the alcohol. **We weren't drinking to spend time together. We were together to have an excuse to drink.**

The realization suffocated me. The air grew hot and stiff and my heart pulsated with the heat. Eventually, the room became so insufferable, I walked outside for some fresh air. Once outside, I kept walking. And walking. And walking. Drunk, I walked in the dark to my host family's home. When I got there, I drifted to sleep. No one cared if I was at the party or in my bed anyways.

As I stumbled down the stairs the next morning, my host mom sat at the kitchen table. Her face had the heart-shattering look of disappointment which only a mom can pull off. She frowned at me and said I shouldn't have left on my own.

Apparently, some of my closest friends had realized I had left the party and told her. She complained about how dangerous my decision had been and how I should have come home with everyone else instead of leaving alone.

But her concern didn't matter to me. The shadow of alcohol had already overtaken every relationship I had in the United States. Alcohol tainted my memories with even my closest friends in America. Besides, most of them saw me as an outcast and foreigner unless there were beers in our hands. I was done caring about people who didn't care about me.

In the United States, I experienced how alcohol distorts relationships, but I didn't take the time to understand it. I didn't yet understand how it shifts the focus off community and belonging and onto fitting in. While sometimes confused as synonymous, belonging and fitting in are two very different things.

When we belong, those around us accept us for who we are. Fitting in is when we change ourselves in order to suit what we think others want us to be. Belonging comes from authenticity and finding our people. Fitting in is a result of changing who we are to fit those already around us. Side effects of fitting in include:

- Feelings of inferiority
- Insecurity
- A lack of confidence in our actions, words, clothing, etc.
- Anxiety
- Not taking risks or getting outside our comfort zone because we're afraid how others will react
- Discomfort sharing thoughts, dreams, or ideas with others or showing our true selves to others
- Conforming to what everyone else is doing, even if it's not what we want to do

When we belong we feel comfortable to:

- Try new things
- Act authentically
- Share our dreams

Belonging = that overwhelming peace and confidence we feel when we're with loved ones and friends who accept us for who we are.

Fitting in = the stress and overwhelm of never feeling like we're enough, especially when we're with others.

Another key difference is who has the power. When we're in a state of belonging, we have the power. We feel like GODs whose opinions and true selves are valued by those around us. When we try to fit in, others have the power–we're obsessed with how others see us.

For a country run on nationalism, the goal is to take away the power of belonging and keep people in a state of fitting in. Teaching people how to fit in from a young age is vital to the survival of those in power. There's very little focus on helping people belong, though there is a lot of effort to create the illusion of belonging. The church, government, and other societal groups that influence the masses often use symbols, traditions, and stories to make people feel like they belong when what the individual is really doing is adjusting their behaviors to fit the agenda of the larger group. Whether we're gathering around a flag or a cross, we have to ask ourselves what is demanded in return for that sense of community.

If community comes with obligations, it's a place where we must fit in. If a community lets us come as we are, it's a place of belonging.

Of course, there is an even darker side to the illusion of belonging, discriminating against those who don't fit in, but we'll get to that in the next chapter. For now, it's best to be aware of what nation-states and religions want from us.

So often, these groups pay us in the illusion of belonging, only asking that we fit in and do as they say in return. The US version of nationalism gets bonus points for getting teenagers to care so much about fitting in, they permanently damage their livers in the process. My time in America taught me how alcohol ruins communities and how nationalism thrives by teaching people the art of sacrifice for the comfort of those around them.

Nationalism is on the rise in almost every nation today and we are often reminded about the sacrifices made by the people that came before us. Nationalistic governments create holidays to remember these sacrifices. They create a culture of thanking those who sacrifice whenever we see them in public, such as armed service members. In essence, the goal is to glamorize sacrifice for the good of the nation, even if the sacrifice includes committing war crimes. The idea is to make people feel like they need to fit in at all costs.

Nationalism creates a contest of who can sacrifice the most to fit in

In this sort of society, we also want other people to suffer like us, for the sake of solidarity. But we are also ready to let other people suffer in our place–or to persecute others unfairly.

Self Discovery Exercise
BEFORE READING THE NEXT CHAPTER,
CHOOSE A COUNTRY.
JOT DOWN WHAT STORIES WERE TOLD ABOUT THIS
COUNTRY'S HISTORY AND PLACE IN THE WORLD.
HOW HAVE THOSE STORIES INFLUESPIRED US AS
WE'VE GROWN UP?

Keep these things in mind as we progress to the next drinking story and another aspect related to nationalism and the persecution it causes.

Chapter 3:
What a Wonderful Brawl

Well, my friends, we are at the third and final part of the society influespire level. First, we looked at religion and how it can take away our ability to be GODs and creators of our realities. Then we looked at the perils of nationalism and how it forces us to fit in instead of belonging to our true selves and a like minded community. Now it's time for a parable... and maybe another drinking story.

A young man went to the same bar in his hometown each weekend and saw the same three people. The three sat next to each other at the bar, but they all looked and sounded different. He would see each as a unique individual with a different way of thinking. One summer, he decided to backpack around Southeast Asia and New Zealand. At the end of the trip, he went back to the bar in his hometown. This time, the three people all had the same energy and felt the same to the man.

While this might seem like a nonsense parable, it does have something to do with the third element of society, discrimination. Stay with me for a bit while I explain this. It demonstrates how division and unity amongst people are subjective and change as we travel further away from home or are exposed to new cultures and experiences.

Often, society divides us into different groups, yet at the end of the day, those divisions are arbitrary.

Throughout the centuries, people have divided themselves up into a variety of categories:

- Racial identity
- Ethnic identity
- Religious affiliation
- Political ideology
- Cat or dog person
- Those who think Rachel and Ross were on a break and those who don't

The last two are more of a joke, though there have been some odd, painful divisions throughout history. During the Cold War, left-handed folks in the United States were considered communists. To make it even more confusing, left-handed people in the Soviet Union were considered capitalists! Throughout history, smaller groups, such as those who practiced a form of "witchcraft," were cast out of communities because they were thought to bring bad luck 😑

Discrimination often starts with the creation of in-groups and out-groups in the society, which create a fake sense of community. When an in-group is formed, those in it are able to bond over an us vs them mindset, similar to two rival sports teams, but with much darker consequences.

An in-group is a group of people who bond over sharing some sort of trait that an in-group has and an out-group doesn't have. For example, if we're in a group of people who all like pizza except one member, Jim, we might form a pizza in-group. The in-group could organize events and have a group chat (without Jim) to discuss the best pizza in town. Eventually, our resentment toward Jim who doesn't like pizza could grow so strong, we glare at him whenever he's around and try to avoid him at all costs. Sorry, Jim.

This can become a harmful phenomenon fast, especially if the classification is around a more contentious trait than pizza, such as race or religion, and if the in-group begins to see themselves as good and the out-group as bad. No one would choose to be discriminated against, but many will discriminate out of fear that if they don't, someone else will put them in an out-group.

In *Man's Search for Meaning* (I highly recommend reading it if the multiple references to it already in this book didn't give that away), Frankl discusses how humans are ultimately divided into two categories: good people and bad people. Yet in society, we make it more complicated and add more divisions. In Nazi Germany, some of the guards at concentration camps took pleasure in punishing others while other guards were kinder, aka they had some sympathy and tried to make it easier for the prisoners without getting in trouble themselves, though sometimes they did risk getting in trouble too.

Among the prisoners, there were two similar groups. Some prisoners would take advantage of the others to create a better situation for themselves, while others would protect fellow prisoners. Frankl's work demonstrates how even though we create divisions in society, there's only one division that matters: if people are good or bad. The rest is pure fiction–and extremely harmful as history shows us time and time again.

Nazi Germany perpetrated monstrous atrocities, but it has not been the only one. Think of the Japanese concentration camps in the United States or the Uyghur internment camps in China, not to mention the Kurds in Turkey, Muslims in India, Indigenous communities in Australia, Desaparecidos in Argentina, Congolese in Congo Free State (probably the worst "country" to ever exist) and so on and on and on... I am afraid the list could fill the entire book.

Much of the world's current conception of discrimination is rooted in the slave trade. Before the slave trade, in-groups and out-groups were more local. Early European communities had in-groups and out-groups in one single country, such as Christians and non-Christians. After the slave trade started, Black and Indigenous people were forced to join European society and were seen as different than the newly constructed idea of Europeans. The Europeans used these new racial constructs to prey on these new groups. Often, Europeans would pay for goods with the trade of slaves because of how othersized Africans were in this new, global society.

The discrimination was so extreme, these communities were no longer considered human, but animals. The religious Europeans and missionaries in other parts of the world pretended to pray for the weak, but they actually preyed on the weak–*flashback to the chapter on religion, anyone?*

And the danger of discrimination isn't in the past, as the Russian assault on Ukraine and the Chinese discrimination against the Uyghurs, a religious minority, show us. Any societal division is faulty and dangerous, past or present. In any other division we create, there will be some good and some bad people, not all good or all bad people.

- Not all priests are good. Some are wonderful while others are criminals.
- Some teachers are decent while others are indecent.
- Some people are in jail for speaking out against a corrupt political system, while others committed rape or murder.

We can replace the divider with anything (lawyers, cooks, whites, Blacks, Christians, Jews, etc.) and there will always be some good and bad individuals in each human-defined category. Yet, we're so desperate for community, we create it in the wrong way: through creating in-groups and out-groups and labeling one group as bad and one as good.

Usually we see those who are the same as us as part of our group and "good" while those we see as different are in an out-group or are "bad." If we think of all lawyers, all people from the US, all Black people, or any other large group, we might have some misconceptions.

For example, a common stereotype about lawyers is that they're all evil and hungry for money, yet many lawyers fight for civil rights or defend innocent people in criminal trials. All or nothing thinking is always problematic!

Whenever we try to classify any group based on profession, race, nationality, or any other trait, there will always be an exception to any stereotype. As much as some try to group us in order to control us, it isn't possible to create a neat in-group with a set of traits which every member has. **People just aren't that simple** 👻

Historically, people have always classified others in an attempt to control them. The ancient Egyptians and Greeks were particularly good at dividing by religion on the outside and social hierarchy on the inside to maintain control. They separated themselves from those who worshiped other Gods and divided into classes those who worshiped the same gods.

By the end of the medieval ages, people were classified by their nation as nationalism rose and wars, such as the 100 year war between France and Britain broke out because of national identity (among land disputes and other causes). As nations were being established, more and more in-groups were created. This now permeates our society in the form of discrimination.

Discrimination, like any other classification, is constructed by our society. While it's inevitable that our cultural background influences our choices and the way we act, it doesn't have to lead to discrimination. Someone who was raised in Africa and identifies as Black will have experienced a very different life than someone who was raised in Alaska and identifies as Indigenous. But these differences are due to upbringing, not because of societal stereotypes or harmful differences.

Defining one's group affiliation is as difficult to grasp as running water in a stream.

The meaning of one "race" or any other group affiliation (such as an ethnic background or occupation) changes drastically throughout time and space. One can be Asian, but being Korean is different from Japanese– some cultures would make the distinction between the two "races" while others wouldn't. If two people are white, they could also be divided into different subraces. One who came from Poland might consider themselves Eastern Europeans while a person from Spain might consider themselves Southern European.

One of the most extreme cases of division is the caste system in India. For many non-Indians, all Indians are the same, but for Indians, what I just said is blasphemy, as everyone knows that being from one caste is different than being from any other caste, even if in reality the castes don't define who someone is as an individual. Unlike racial stereotypes, these castes are decided by a number of arbitrary effects, though the result is still the same: discrimination.

If we look at discrimination on the third influespire level, society, we can see how our idea of society also influences what we think about race. In a small society, like Alvada, there is less diversity so some people discriminated against me. As an Italian, some considered me "non-white" as I was not "American-white," but this is unlikely to happen in a big city like New York or Amsterdam. This is because I was different from the people they were used to seeing, whereas New York or Amsterdam would have a wider variety of people, making it more difficult to stand out and be discriminated against (but not impossible!).

The more cultures we interact with and people we meet, the less we'll worry about the differences. That's why it's important to broaden our horizons–meeting people and exploring cultures can change our entire perspective.

That being said (and I promise I'm not trying to 100% contradict myself), our identity and cultural and racial connections do influence how we perceive the world. They are often one of the biggest factors on all three influespire levels. They determine who is allowed in our community or pack and who isn't. They can even wrongly dictate how we treat others or how we perceive others.

Today, our communities are divided into several geographic boxes with multiple levels. Think of Matryoshka dolls or Chinese boxes. These can include states, counties, cities, regions, and more. People living within each "box" and "level" feel a sense of fitting into many particular in-groups based on the context they are facing at any given moment.

The further away someone is from our most immediate box (our town or city), the more distant we might feel from them compared to someone in a closer in-group, unless we are temporarily identifying ourselves with that further out in-group. After all, the most hated player from the rival team all of a sudden becomes our hero when playing for the national team.

Of course, this is in no way prescriptive or always the case–though we all know the stereotypes of others around us, such as the town next door that's too snobby or the bordering state which is "poorer" and less hardworking than us.

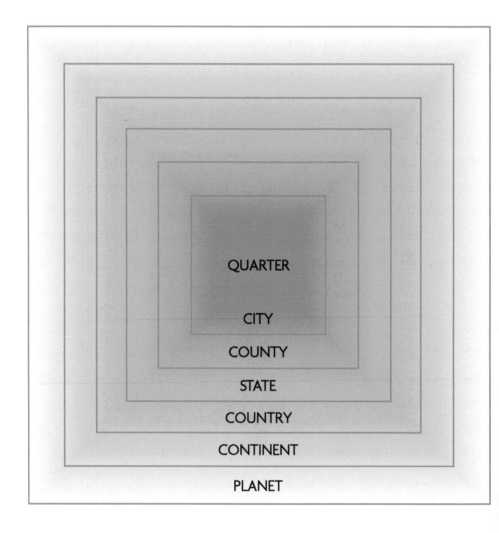

QUARTER

CITY

COUNTY

STATE

COUNTRY

CONTINENT

PLANET

To make this (hopefully) less confusing, I'll use my own boxes as an example. Again, I'm hoping to make it less confusing, though Italy is known for creating some wild boxes. Here's what my boxes would look like for reference:

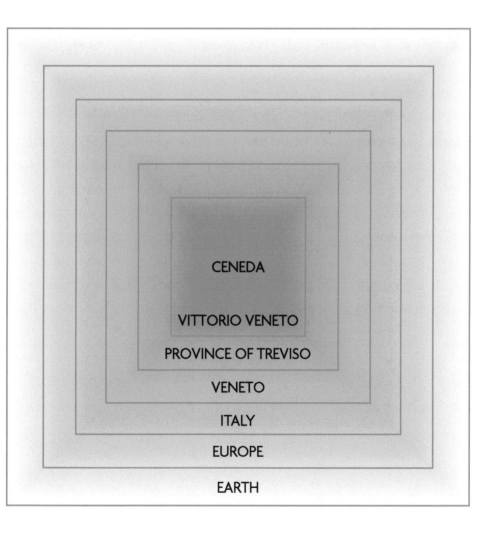

CENEDA

VITTORIO VENETO

PROVINCE OF TREVISO

VENETO

ITALY

EUROPE

EARTH

I am from Ceneda which is one of the two historical towns, the other being Serravalle, that formed Vittorio Veneto over 150 years ago. Ceneda is divided between Alta and Bassa (High and Low) and obviously people from Alta, where I am from, are better than folks from Bassa. No need to ask anyone from Bassa about this! My wife's main flaw was being from the wrong side of town. The moment we start dealing with people from Conegliano, which is a city south of Vittorio Veneto, then all of a sudden the people from Serravalle become good as well, because no one is as bad as the Coneglianesi.

Zooming out a bit more, the Province of Treviso, where both Conegliano and Vittorio Veneto are, is the best province in Veneto, much better than Padova, Venezia, Belluno, Verona, Vicenza or Rovigo. No one really likes Rovigo anyways since it is just a foggy swamp. Veneto is the best region in northern Italy (even if the picture doesn't show it), because Lombardy is too debauched, Piedmont is too aristocratic, Valle d'Aosta is too small, Liguria is too tight, Emilia-Romagna is too communist, Friuli is too backward, and Trentino Alto Adige is not even Italy.

But northern Italy is the best! The center and the south are just sucking away all the wealth produced in the north and doing nothing all day, basking in the sun.

Yet Italians are the best in the world, and not just in football! We are the best lovers, have the best cars, and are the most fashionable. Plus, who can argue against Italian food being the best cuisine in the world?

We can all use a similar visualization to reflect on how this impacts our lives.

Self Discovery Exercise
FILL IN THE BOXES.
JOT DOWN THREE DIFFERENT IDENTITIES AND WHAT STEREOTYPES THERE ARE AROUND THEM.
DO THESE ALWAYS STACK UP?
HOW CAN WE MORE EFFECTIVELY FIGHT AGAINST THESE STEREOTYPES?

Now that we've discussed in-groups on a bigger scale, let's dive into that small Italian town of Ceneda, circa 1989. A couple of weeks before my thirteenth birthday, my parents separated and my father left the house, leaving my mother with three children: me and my eleven-year-old and four-month-old brothers. Not that my father was present before then (he constantly traveled for work) but at least he was there, a form of authority. Everyone is supposed to have a father figure in their family, even if the figure only appears that way and doesn't act like it.

With him gone and my mother busy with my newborn brother, I had freedom to do whatever I wanted. Being the better behaved of the two older brothers, I enjoyed the luxury of no supervision whatsoever. A good, stable family allows us a safe, certain childhood, but it also has its downsides, with a relative lack of freedom being one of them.

Our family, if we have one, is the strongest element of the second level of influespire, as it heavily influences any of us from day one and for a very long period of time–and we'll discuss this more later in the book. For now, let's get back to the story.

My friends and I spent our weekends drinking wine and talking between the ages of fourteen and sixteen. We would sit on the stairs of the church and do nothing but chat, watching as the city, cars, and time passed by. Back then, there was nothing better to do than spend time with our friends.

The teenage years are the six years in our lives during which we are expected to transform from children into adults. Some of us manage, some of us don't. By thirteen, I was far from an adult but I had the freedom to drink whatever I wanted when I wanted. I didn't abuse it as during my time in America, but I for sure drank more than I was supposed to at that age.

A usual thing to do back then was to help a friend of mine to bottle the wine his father would purchase. In Veneto, we bought wine in demijohns and decanted it into bottles, as it was way cheaper than buying the bottles directly.

We would pump the wine out of the demijohn into the bottles and, in the process, drink at least a bottle of wine, as we would pass the pump between us while we handled the different bottles. It was always great fun and I always ended up half drunk.

Insane Drinking Wisdom
*SAVE MONEY **BY BULK BUYING WINE AND DRINK WHILE DECANTING SO THE PROCESS IS** MORE FUN*.

At fourteen, I started high school, though I luckily didn't run into any mean girls with a Burn Book. That same year, a new pizza place opened in front of the school. It was a new joint set up by the same family who had a very popular pizzeria in town. They spent a few months preparing the new location and set a date for the big opening.

My classmate, who later in life became my best man, and I decided to go to the opening as it was an event not to be missed. For an occasion like this, it was normal to give away free drinks and food, so that the community would go there and get to know the new restaurant and owners.

We kept on drinking and eating as if there was no tomorrow—after all, free food and drinks always go down even when we are not hungry or thirsty. After a while we were surprisingly able to secure a place at a small table in a corner, so we sat down with our beers and continued enjoying ourselves. By the time his father came to pick us up, my teeth were feeling large(ish), making the car ride home a rollercoaster.

When I came back from America, it was odd for me to drink with my friends in the same way I used to. Like the young man in the parable at the beginning of this chapter, I saw the differences between the people at the bar before I traveled.

However, when I returned, everyone surrounding me seemed the same. The young man saw differences between the people at the bar until he traveled because the travel skewed his perception of who was alike and who was different.

Similarly, half of Vittorio Veneto was at the restaurant opening and they all looked different to me before I left for the United States. But my travels had shifted my perspective of those around me. When we travel, we're exposed to different ways of living and cultures other than our own. We broaden our horizons and it changes the way we look at things for the better.

We are born and raised into our religion, nation, and societal stereotypes, and they play such a big role in our lives–even though we can easily shift what each means and what it means to be a part of each group.

When we don't question the third level, we confine ourselves to the fictional boxes they cast over our lives. From the confines of these boxes we act as agents of discrimination against those we see as lesser for no good reason.

When we do question them, we can see how subjective they are and that the reality around us is not one dimensional. Seeing these differences is the first step toward making decisions as an individual, not as products of our societies.

We are all humans, no matter what society we grew up in. The easiest way to confront this discrimination is to face it within ourselves and be in a state of growth, learning about new cultures and perspectives whenever possible.

Self Discovery Exercise

CONSIDERING THE ENTIRE THIRD LEVEL OF INFLUESPIRE AS DESCRIBED IN THESE INITIAL CHAPTERS, JOT DOWN *1-3 EXTERNAL SOCIETAL FACTORS* THAT STILL IMPACT INDIVIDUALS.

HOW DO THESE FACTORS ASK US TO GIVE UP OUR POWER OR LOOK FOR VALIDATION *OUTSIDE OURSELVES?*

Regardless of our race, nationality, religion, or sex (all things we have done nothing to achieve, other than being born), we need to work on ourselves to truly understand who we are.

I was born a catholic Italian white man, but I am none of those things today. I don't feel like any of those, and I don't allow them to define me.

When we decide to look past the groups given to us by society, we can see the people underneath. We wholeheartedly can feel the truth: we are all human.

Our race, sex, religion, or nationality don't define us. Our humanness does.

However, there's no point in simply refusing these identities to escape our responsibility. Our societies' dangerous flaws, including discrimination against others or identifying too much with one group, lead to loneliness, abuse, and even murder.

When we ignore the harm nationalism, religious extremism, and discrimination cause, we can't play our part in finding a better way to organize ourselves. A way where we collectively let go of the negative influences poured on us by the third level of influespire and focus on their positive inspirations.

We need a new way of working together in unison to create a shared, peaceful, and safe reality. We need to learn to flip the script–to love one another no matter how "different" someone else might be.

And working together we must, like we are about to see as we leap into our pack, the second influespire level. Follow me ⊘

Chapter 4:
Drinking Class Hero

In the beginning, there was work. While it might not be as inevitable as death and taxes, most people have worked in order to live for most of human history. Work is necessary and always has been, even if (and often especially when) we dread it.

But we didn't always dread work–and it's possible for most to do what we like, or even love, for a living! It is possible to wake up excited on a Monday morning, eager for the tasks ahead. We all can find a career path where we don't cringe when someone asks what we do for a living. And, most importantly, we can feel those 30-50 hours we spend working a week are making the world a better place.

But before we reveal how to find work we love, let's examine what work is and how we got to a point where over half of us hate our jobs (the global percentage of how many people hate work is between 55-85%, depending on the poll). First things first, let's check in on what we already know.

WHY DO WE WORK?
WRITE DOWN ANY POSSIBLE REASONS OR IDEAS OF HOW OUR IDEA OF WORK EVOLVED OVER TIME.

Let's take it back to the beginning... or at least 30,000 years ago. Back then, humans worked, though it might have looked a bit different than how we write about our role on LinkedIn. First, people worked out of necessity. The output of their labor was food to eat, fire to keep them warm, and weapons and skills to protect themselves from other creatures.

The two jobs early humans could choose between were hunters and gatherers, though often everyone would do both despite what was in the job description (something many of us can relate to today). Humans got so good at protecting themselves and providing food, they killed off many other large animals and drove numerous species to extinction.

As we evolved, we continued to work more as a community, shifting from clans, to tribes, to cities (remember the picture in chapter 0?), and easing the individual burden to provide the bare necessities. Early civilizations, such as Mesopotamia, formed. In these ancient societies, many new jobs besides hunting and gathering popped up–the first being farming. When farming became efficient, people worked in other fields like entertainment and trade. Others built sturdy shelters so humans no longer had to sleep in caves and shelters.

These new societies had leadership roles to keep society functioning and economic classes formed based on how big of a leadership role one had–and thus how big their salary was. As we became more sedentary with farming, we developed better control over our food chain and invented many new foods like bread, cheese and also alcohol, which led to new jobs as baker, cheesemaker, or brewer.

Societies grew larger yet again (think Ancient Egypt and Ancient Rome) and there were even more new jobs than before. Being a soldier, a politician, a scholar, and an artist became more prevalent and sought-after. In the upper echelons of these societies, some decided they didn't want to work at all and outsourced even personal tasks like getting dressed to slaves and servants. It also led to more free time for the ultra wealthy and skilled workers–time that could be spent coming up with new drinks. From the days of Ancient Egypt, these wines and beers were given to every social class.

Outsourcing remained a way for the rich to avoid work as the medieval and renaissance eras brought feudal societies. Much of the work in these societies focused on agriculture and most workers lived together in agricultural communities. This led to food surpluses, and jobs in specific crafts and arts became more common. Of course, people had even more time for dancing on tables, drinking mead, and fighting each other at the local tavern.

The industrial revolution disrupted work once again. Craftsmen were replaced by machines and guilds had to take up work in the much more efficient factories. Agricultural inventions also made that industry more effective and put many farmers out of work. These farmers migrated to cities for jobs in factories alongside former guild members. Because work in the factories was long and consuming, workers usually didn't have the time or energy for hobbies. What's one hobby that doesn't take a lot of upfront time and gives short-term energy? Drinking. Drinking until drunk became more popular, despite the efforts of temperance movements.

As many of us know, the conditions in these factories were lackluster and many pushed for better working conditions and a 40 hour work week. Many of these requests were granted over time and, as factories became more efficient, more people migrated to office jobs or running small businesses. Of course, a love of alcohol remained.

Computers and the internet revolutionized work once again... and not always for the best. It's now almost impossible to unplug from work and there's always something else we could be doing. Unless we throw our phones and laptops out the window and escape to a remote location, our bosses and clients can most likely contact us anytime of the day.

Similar to during the industrial revolution, this change has led people to reconsider work/life balance. The younger generations now ask for more vacation time, a transition to a four day work week, and to be put on projects they are passionate about, rather than doing mindless repetitive tasks. We've created the concept of having a job we love and set that as the golden standard. Whether we should be looking for a job we love or one we can tolerate which respects our boundaries is a different discussion.

We now look for fulfilling jobs which can change the world, not just pay the bills 💰 Ironically, as more of us look for a passion-filled job, the fewer of us feel satisfied at work, probably because it's harder than ever before to see a direct impact from our work. Before, our work on the farm or even in a small, local business had a direct impact on our friends' and family's lives. Today, many of us sit in an office looking at spreadsheets for eight hours a day and it's hard to experience the impact from that work.

Despite the lack of impact we feel from our work, almost everyone alive today works and most aim to make more and more money, all while on the quest for the elusive dream job. We no longer work in exchange for food and basic necessities, instead we work for titles and salaries that give us admiration and respect amongst our peers. We work in hopes that it will bring meaning to our lives–and sometimes because emails and work projects are an escape when our emotions are too hard to process. We buy people's time and allow others to buy our time in order to be able to pay for a lifestyle everyone says we should have.

During my career, I've experienced how easy it is to get sucked into work for money, drowning in spreadsheets and meetings instead of changing the world. At 28, when I moved to the UK, I got one of my first office jobs and I was so excited about the opportunity to explore a new culture and role at work. I didn't realize my love affair with alcohol was excited about the move too.

My time in the UK was full of nonsensical drinking which would sometimes pour over into violence. The British added a new dimension to drinking that I had never experienced in Italy or the US: violence. In Italy, I never saw a fight between drunk people (not to say that they don't happen). In the UK, I saw it every weekend.

Every hobby, work event, and weekend out involved drinking, often heavily. Even sports clubs, such as the friend group I climbed with on Tuesday and Thursday nights, would drink together. Thursday nights were the best climbing club nights because we drank at the pubs down at the harbor after climbing. Despite work the next day, the pubs flowed with professionals on any weeknight.

Fridays and Saturdays were even wilder. Ambulances waited on the street because people passing out from drinking was a nightly routine. And it wasn't just college kids getting black out drunk and fighting. Even at work parties, people would drink as much as they could on the company dime. Any company that had an alcohol free party might have been reported for abusing their employees!

One week, my coworkers and I arranged an unforgettable night out, even though I can only remember parts of it. We ventured down to a comedy club in a boat on the Thames which charged 20 pounds for a comedy show without revealing who the audience would see. It could be a famous comedian testing new material or someone no one had heard of–and never would hear of again. That night, we had some extremely popular comedians: Eddie Izzard, Alan Carr, Greg Davis and Russell Kane 😂

The 20 of us got on the boat, bought a couple of drinks, and spent the night laughing at the comedians' jokes and with each other. Every time one of the comedians came out, it was a surprise. They were all so high profile!

After the show, we had more drinks and the boat transformed from a comedy club to a dance floor–DJ included. Some of us drank less, some of us drank more. I'll let others decide which category I fell into.

Insane Drinking Wisdom

WORK **HARD,** PLAY **HARDER...** IDEALLY DRUNK AND WITH OUR COWORKERS.

At the end of the night, we took the metro toward Liverpool Street Station. I stood on the metro until it swayed. Dizzy and with my teeth large, the alcohol bubbled up within me and made it impossible to be in a confined, crowded space. Those around me sucked all the oxygen out of the air and I had to leave before it became impossible to breathe. As the doors were closing, I jumped out of the metro, relieved not to be boxed into a metal cylinder full of people. But I was leaving my gasping colleagues, who knew that was my last chance out of the city.

Alone, I left the tube station and walked around the block, trying to clear my head even as the alcohol made me stumble with each step. When I got to the station, it was closed and wouldn't open again until 5am. In the four hours I had to kill, I walked around the city drunk (including in some areas no one wants to be in after dark).

By 2am, I staggered, completely drunk, down the street. Everyone gave the swaggering drunk room–even the vagabonds stayed away from me. At one point, I was so drunk, I walked onto the London Overground tracks. My drunk self thought I could walk the tracks back to my home. Obviously, I didn't make it. I only managed to fall and cut my hand.

Luckily, I got off the metro tracks before the trains started running again. The details are fuzzy, but I somehow managed to find my way back to Liverpool Street Station right around 5am–and I know GPS wasn't how I did this as smartphones weren't a thing yet. Completely tired from the sleepless night walking around Bethnal Green, I went to the first train leaving for home.

While I managed to get home safely, that night represents how many of us accidentally go through life: blundering drunkenly without a clear idea of how to get home; in our career, home often looks like a job making an impact and pursuing our dreams.

When others' ideas of what work should look like infiltrate our mind, we are metaphorically drunk. If we design our work life around what other people say will create success, we will do what it takes to fit in. The bubbly feeling of promotions and pay raises will keep us performing according to someone else's standards instead of arriving home. Over time, we'll end up alone, lost, hurt, and unsure of how we got to where we are or how to get home.

In a more literal sense, I drank to fit in that night in London. I loved the bubbly recognition and kept drinking, praying for the feeling to never leave me. Eventually, I found myself walking alone, black out drunk and lost. And the modern working world makes it easy to stumble drunkenly throughout our entire careers, from college to retirement–and one heck of a hangover if we live and work wrong!

Even when we study, most of us will choose "safe" majors that allow us to make more money, like finance or software engineering, instead of ones we are actually passionate about, like history, art, or philosophy. While I first wanted to study astronomy, my parents made me choose the more safe civil engineering program. And I hated it. Before wasting too much time in the program (and getting more failed grades like I had that first semester) I dropped out. Because of dropping out, I couldn't postpone the mandatory military service and had to join the army.

Since I didn't enjoy my time in the army, it gave me the motivation to study something that would allow me to have a career. After graduating with a degree in economics, I got a safe, well-paid finance job and the money allowed me to achieve many of my dreams, such as having a family, buying a house, and traveling.

I got very good at my job in risk management and it became easy to make money by not following the rules of work. Had I pushed through that first degree, I would be living someone else's dream as an engineer, simply because I thought that would mean I was successful.

No matter what we do for a living, there are two ways to work:

- Working by the conventional rules and playing it safe whenever possible 😥
- Challenging the rules of our organizations and staying true to ourselves 😤

The second option is better for ourselves, those around us, and even the companies we work for as it creates innovation and pushes us to do our best. It comes with excitement, leadership, and the thrill of overcoming challenges. But the first category is less risky–it offers stability, and the peace of not challenging the status quo and not taking too much initiative on projects. Both ways work for different people, there is no absolute right and wrong.

Even for those who work the second way and go after work they love, jobs can leave us stumbling around the streets of London, drunk and exhausted (metaphorically, hopefully). For me, this metaphorical drunkenness looked like my workload consuming any time with my family or for my passions. I got bored of the same routine I had once loved, which is why I resigned from a high-paying job and started over.

In fairness, I have always resigned from all of my jobs, as the passion that got me into them faded away over time. I had consumed the "novelty" and learned what I had to learn, and so the only thing to do was to move on... before the inevitable downturn caught up with me and made me hate my jobs.

But after that last resignation from said high-paying job, I became a consultant and business owner instead of taking on a new role. I redesigned my work/life balance to include more life and to only take on meaningful work.

To give us a better idea of how to find the way to a healthier relationship with work, let's take a look at my own career. I have had my fair share of working both ways–and mistakes and misdirections along the way.

At age 19, I made my way into the workforce with a peach of a job: working at a fruit and veggie stand. Within one week, I realized it was not the job for me. Talking to customers and convincing them to buy fruits and veggies made me squirm, not to mention the dread of annoyed customers.

Sidenote: If everyone worked in a service industry for at least six months, the world would be a better place.

After that experience, I had to find a job that wasn't public facing–any crazy person can walk through a shop door. Since I was still in university and my resume could fit on one grape from my previous job, I took any work I could find–factories, warehouses, moving companies. During this time, I even worked in a distillery where we distilled the pomace (aka the leftovers of wine production) into grappa. As if alcohol wasn't already such a dominant presence in my life 😅

None of those jobs was a match made in heaven, but they all gave me something valuable: feedback on what I didn't want. During the odd jobs of my early 20s, I recognized the value of a job done with passion. I rolled up my sleeves, studied harder, and dreamed of what my stable, fulfilling career in economics would look like after graduating.

Like any good dream, it took a while to get there. When I first graduated, my then girlfriend/now wife and I moved to the United Kingdom for her work. I applied to every job I could find within my field in the UK. But without any relevant work experience and a generic economics university degree, I didn't get any response whatsoever. I was an immigrant who could say ciao and head home at any time–not exactly a combo lots of employers were eager to hire and invest in.

After months applying for jobs, the Christmas season started and the royal post office needed extra workers to sort the mail. To ensure I got the job, I applied for the dreaded night shift. For six weeks, my nights belonged to sorting the mail and my days to sleeping.

One day, I trained a new employee about how to stamp the envelopes correctly. He couldn't figure it out, even after my instruction.
That's when I knew I needed to improve my communication. I had to learn how to make sure everyone knew what we were doing instead of acting on confused assumptions.

After the post office, I got a job selling advertisements. I hated it, but it was my first office job, and it was instrumental to catching the dreaded 22: having six months of working experience before anyone would even think to extend an offer for an entry-level job. Once I got six months with them I applied to other jobs again and got called immediately for the job. That next job became my entire career: **risk management.**

In 2007, I got a "big boy" job in payments, despite being the most entry-level job there was. At first I worked with money, which was always something that interested me. However, my real interest wasn't in money itself but how money can transfer value between two people. If we don't want to go back to a barter society where one person gives someone else a carrot for a tomato, we need money (like it or not) and understanding how that money moved throughout society fascinated me.

Money often gets a bad rep. People manipulate others with the power of money, they flaunt their wealth which others don't have, and we all have nervously checked our bank statements. But money is just a tool, not evil in and of itself. I wanted to pivot into a career where I could help others see the value of money too.

As I previously mentioned, I would resign and move on to a new job whenever the current one wasn't challenging enough. After my first three years, three promotions, and working in multiple departments in the UK, I was promoted to manager and was sent to the Netherlands.

In my first two or three years in the Netherlands, I learned something new every day. But it was my responsibility whenever I felt stuck to move on to a new job. One day, I walked into my manager's office and said, "I really like my job, but I'm starting to feel like I need something different. Is there anything else for me? If not, I'll move on and find another job."

I carried this transparency–and challenge to the status quo–with me throughout my career and it was always well received. Eventually, I found my way into the ecommerce world. Knowing what I wanted helped me pick my job with a global payment service provider. With this job, I traveled all over the world and learned about how finance and payments interact with different cultures. My approach was listening, learning, and trying to understand how things worked and adapting my approach to the needs at hand.

When I transitioned from credit risk management to more generic risk management, it made sense. Risk management allowed me to make recommendations about how financial payment software could avoid dangers and harms so our customers could have the best payment experience possible. This would allow the customers to look more favorably on not only the companies I worked for, but the exchange of money within our society.

Risk management also made sense for my personality. Even with all my drunk nights, I never once got into a fight. I could always smell trouble from a mile away–risk management has always been a talent in me. If someone is doing something which is too hard for them, it's probably not right for them. The various service and industrial jobs I worked were hard, but working in finance came easier to me.

That job exhausted its appeal in 2019, and for the first time I did not know what to do next, other than not another job in risk management or payments. However, because I was so far into my career and people knew my experience was in risk management for payment services, companies came to me only for services in those fields, like how an actor gets typecast for a character in a hit TV show and can't find any different work after.

Because I still needed to make money, I took another job–which was the worst of all my finance jobs. It was a corporate setting and few employees had a genuine drive to go above and beyond. Luckily, I realized the company culture right away and on day 49, I resigned. I gave up without a backup plan–and sat around my house for quite a while afterward.

After a couple of months on a break, considering what I wanted to do, I went into consultancy. Many people came looking for my services since I had developed a good reputation over my career. In my consultancy role, I could choose my work experience, when (and for how long) I went on vacation, and what my day-to-day looked like. Three years later, I work less and make more than at any full-time job I've had. This new reality would have been unfathomable to me five years earlier.

If I had stuck with the first way of working, which I did before graduating college, I wouldn't be where I am today. I wouldn't have left each job when it became less challenging. I wouldn't have pushed myself and the companies I work for to do better. I wouldn't be sitting here writing this book.

If a job makes us go crazy or is boring, we are doing the wrong thing. Not only that, but too many people who are unhappy in their jobs have the expectation that their boss or HR will change the environment for them. They don't think to take proactive actions to change the environment or themselves. And this initiative to be proactive needs to go beyond the work we do, which is only half of our career. The other half is how aligned we feel with the workplace culture.

The quickest way to make a toxic work culture is to do things for others only if they do something for us first. Throughout my career, I have seen many people try to act out of spite, network with people only to get something from them, or only do someone a favor to "balance the score."

Think about how we feel when someone acts this way toward us–not good. But the only way toxic, icky feelings can leave the workplace is if we're the ones to take the first step. No one, not even HR, can create a cultural shift alone–we have to be a part of the movement. Bonus points if we can be leaders in shifting our workplaces to a culture of love, not reciprocity.

When we do change the work culture or what our day-to-day looks like and still feel unchallenged, it's often best to look for a new opportunity. We learn more by giving it up, confronting the fears of unemployment, and learning how to pursue what we actually want. Just like how society moves in cycles, our jobs and the ways we make money move in cycles too–and what comes up must come down.

Even if we turn our passions into our jobs, we will still fall prey to the cycle of ups and downs. They say when one turns their passion into a job, they never have to work a day in their life. This is a double edged sword.

Let's say someone quit a safe job to become a wedding photographer. This had been a dream they had worked toward for their entire lives and shooting photos–creating art!–for a living felt like the best job ever. They got to help people capture special moments while pursuing what they loved.

Yet over time, the work drained them. The weddings blurred together, the weekends sacrificed to receptions and ceremonies grew, and they had a bit too much sand in their apartment from all the beach weddings. They found they were no longer passionate about shooting weddings, but wanted to do more artistic photography. They wanted to create something that would hang in a modern art museum, not a newlyweds' apartment. So, they reinvented their job again.

When we realize that what we once wanted no longer fits our lives, it can be easy to bury our head in the sand and pretend it's still great. But we should never stick with work that doesn't fulfill us anymore–or a bad boss or abusive clients. By sticking around, we aren't solving the problem. We are digging our own grave.

When boredom seeps into work, find something else. Let the cycle flow as designed and go to the next phase of professional and personal evolution. The key here is to find something where the difficulties challenge us, but don't break us. We want work where we don't know all the answers, but which allows us to relax when we aren't working instead of feeling stressed about tomorrow. Whenever possible, it should also align with our dreams slightly more than the last job.

TO HELL *FIND A JOB* OR WAY OF MAKING MONEY THAT FITS THOSE CRITERIA, *CONSIDER COMPLETING THE FOLLOWING* SELF DISCOVERY EXERCISE:

- **Jot down any passions.**

  This could be anything ranging from claymation to renovating old houses.

- **Brainstorm any jobs that might work for those passions.**

  For example, if one loves to ski, a job that might correlate to that passion is becoming a ski instructor or more easily work as a waiter at a ski resort to have the chance to ski every day and feel that love within themselves. Other times, it's not that simple. If someone loves research and keeping up with the Kardashians and other celebrities, being a data analyst for a tabloid or developing an app for other fans might be a great fit.

- **Write any action steps to get closer to that passion being a job.**

  The person who loves to ski could create a weekend to-do list that looked like researching different resorts that were hiring, finding current ski school owners they could conduct informational interviews with, and researching what sort of certifications they need to teach.

Dreams require work, so rinse and repeat these three steps anytime we feel unfulfilled at work or a new dream becomes a call pulling us away from our day-to-day life. While it can be scary to change, the scariest things come when we resist the cycle of change and stay, ignoring our feelings and rejecting our dreams. Like a beautiful dance, the beauty is in the motion. And that motion is more beautiful when we let love lead the way.

Speaking of scary, did we ever discuss the time my friends and I almost destroyed another friend at his graduation's party? Well... let's discuss that, and friendship, in the next chapter

Chapter 5:
Brews've Got a Friend in Me

Want to live longer? Spend more time with friends 👬 (feel free to cite this chapter when choosing to be with loved ones instead of working– this is actual research-backed advice).

At first read, this might sound outlandish, but friendships actually make us healthier, according to recent research. Multiple studies have shown those with stronger friendships experience better mental health, more energy, and a stronger immune system. In fact, friendships can even increase our life expectancy! And being lonely is as damaging to our longevity as smoking a pack of cigarettes a day.

At our core, humans are social animals. We need more than just food to sustain ourselves. And while the third influespire level, society, is important, the second influespire level, our pack, plays a more prominent role in our lives.

In fact, researchers have developed a wheel of well-being that can measure how satisfied someone is with their life. Of the eight elements in this wheel, one directly has to do with friendships. At least five of the others (environmental, physical, emotional, intellectual, and spiritual) are greatly influenced by those closest to us. An argument could be made that our friends influence any and all spheres of well-being.

Using this as an inspiration, I created the stars of wellness, which can be seen below:

Area	Description	Stars
Emotional	How do we feel about our mental health and current emotional state?	☆ ☆ ☆ ☆ ☆
Environmental	Do we feel comfortable and safe within our home and other frequent environments (city, office, etc.)?	☆ ☆ ☆ ☆ ☆
Physical	How happy are we with our level of physical activity and nutrition?	☆ ☆ ☆ ☆ ☆
Financial	How do we feel about our current financial situation?	☆ ☆ ☆ ☆ ☆
Social	How happy are we with our social life, including friends, family, and romantic partner(s)?	☆ ☆ ☆ ☆ ☆
Intellectual	Do we feel intellectually stimulated on a weekly basis?	☆ ☆ ☆ ☆ ☆
Career	How satisfied are we with our current role and where our career is going?	☆ ☆ ☆ ☆ ☆
Spiritual	How fulfilled and at peace do we feel with the universe, or whatever we believe in?	☆ ☆ ☆ ☆ ☆

Self Discovery Exercise

RATE EACH CATEGORY ON A SCALE OF 1-5
AND FILL IN THE NUMBER OF STARS
THAT CORRESPONDS TO THE NUMBER
FOR EACH CATEGORY.

THE AREA WITH THE MOST STARS IS THE STRONGEST
AND SHOULD BE LEVERAGED,
WHILE THE AREA WITH FEWER REQUIRES
MORE ATTENTION AND EFFORT.

Of course, one could argue any close relationship, from coworkers to family members, can influence these aspects of our well-being too. What sets friends apart is that we actively chose them, they actively chose us, and often, they introduce us to entirely new worlds.

If we refer back to the stars, we can brainstorm how friends might positively impact almost every aspect:

- Obviously, they enhance our social life and provide emotional comfort and connection.
- Beyond that, the right friends can be spiritual buddies to meditate, practice yoga, or hike with.
- They can make our environment more livable, especially if they are roommates or they travel with us.
- Friends can be workout buddies and can hold us accountable for leading healthier lives.
- They can also stimulate us intellectually by discussing books, ideas, and life philosophies with us.
- If our friends are career driven or good with finances, they could inspire us to get our finances in order.

The flipside if we make the wrong friends is that they can negatively impact every area of wellness:

- Friends who draw out our insecurities make our social lives hard to bear and harm our emotional well-being.
- Living or traveling with bad friends can make our homes unbearable and full of toxic energy.

- The wrong friends could make fun of us for learning new skills, reading books, or doing other activities which help us thrive cognitively, making us less likely to engage in these activities.
- Friends who prefer to drink instead of going to the gym can harm our physical well-being.
- If we are constantly drinking and partying with our friends, our financial health decreases too and we might be more groggy and perform poorly at work.

The right and wrong friendships can transform our lives. To illustrate how our friends impact us, it's time for a drinking story about one of my best friends, Gorilla 🦍

I first met him when I was fourteen. He wasn't one of the twenty neighborhood kids I hung out with, but instead lived outside of the center of Vittorio Veneto. He lived south of the city and drove to school on a moped. The moped automatically gave him the status of the coolest kid around. Everyone wanted to be his friend and for some reason, he signaled me out as his partner in crime right away. As he assimilated into my friend group, he had to have a nickname. Because he was so hairy–and we were teenage boys–we nicknamed him Gorilla.

Gorilla and I were the best of friends until I went to America. During high school, I had an on-again, off-again girlfriend. The relationship was entirely nonsensical, but my first love, while blind, was also precious to me. Part of the reason this relationship was on-again, off-again was because my girlfriend had a wandering eye. Guys gravitated toward her and every once in a while, she'd leave me for one. I figured some guys would try to flirt with her when I was gone, but I never expected any of my friends to do so.

While in the US, I did cheat on my girlfriend with some girl she'd never meet. At the same time, Gorilla pursued my girlfriend. The first night back in Italy, my girlfriend and I went on a romantic dinner. Later that week, the three of us were at a party. Gorilla saw us kissing, pulled me aside, and told me everything. He said he now realized he had no chance, given the passionate make-out session.

His words, while playful, drove a dagger through my heart. How could my best friend flirt with my girl while I was halfway around the world? Funny enough, I confronted Gorilla about it and while it was a tough conversation, discussing his flirtations with my girlfriend actually brought us closer together. By college, we were roommates.

But we couldn't room together the entire time at college because his degree was longer than mine. Gorilla was studying to be an engineer, one of the most intensive programs in Italy. It's an extremely intensive program which requires students to say goodbye to their social life and any hobbies in exchange for five to eight years of study. In Italy, we say an engineer has the flexibility of granite because by the end of their studies, their minds are so rigid. Things have to be a certain way and there's no discussion about it. If I studied something for eight years, I'd want to be pretty sure it was the way the world actually worked too!

After seven years of crying, stress, and late nights, Gorilla finally graduated from one of the most prestigious engineering programs in Italy.

When Gorilla graduated, we watched his ceremony on video since only the family could go to the in-person ceremony. He invited us to a traditional Italian graduation party after the ceremony. His closest friends decorated a small room with a giant poster of the graduate and we all wrote a long poem, an ode to the person graduating that was full of jokes and innuendos. These poems were never warm and fuzzy. They were similar to what we today would call a roast, except the person graduating had to read the poem to their family and friends.

During the speech, the graduate is undressed by their friends. Most of my graduating friends, and me included, were dressed down to just our underwear 😑

Because of his nickname, we glued more hair onto his body with honey. To add an extra smidge of immaturity, we added a giant inflatable cock to his head. Even his glass (which functioned more like a baby bottle, to be honest) was in the shape of a cock so he sucked prosecco from a cock all night.

Afterward, we moved on to a more formal party organized and paid for by Gorilla's family. They provided a large buffet and drinks for all of us. Our friend washed off the hair beforehand, of course. At the party, already half drunk, we thought it was a great idea to play some drinking games.

One of the other graduates, Churro, joined us. He had no friends or family there and none of us knew him except Gorilla. It was as if he wanted no one to know he graduated–or maybe studying late nights hit him so hard, his degree ruined his social life. After the buffet, we kept drinking at a less formal setting and someone grabbed a whip. The partygoers took turns hitting Gorilla with it. Whenever he had a few too many hits, someone would whip Churro.

I took pity and didn't touch or whip Gorilla all day. Instead, I looked after him, making sure the abuse didn't go too far. Of course, I also drank, took pictures, and enjoyed myself.

Eventually the revelry got out of hand and someone decided it was a good idea to give him an armpit waxing. Other friends shaved off bits and pieces of his hair, until his head looked like a checkerboard of black hair and bald patches. An eyebrow also disappeared. After his haircut, Gorilla passed out. We carried him throughout the city as we bar hopped. He sat at each bar, almost always completely passed out.

Even though he was unconscious, friends kept beating and whipping him. By the end, both Gorilla and Churro had to limp home and sleep on a couch. Bruises and gashes covered their skin and they didn't recover for weeks–even though Churro had his first job interview a couple of days after graduation.

While I would never–under any circumstances–recommend this graduation tradition, it does serve as a look into what our friendships can look like. When troubles arise in our lives, most people we know are our fair weather friends. They either leave or pick up the whip and join the hate against us. Some will even laugh and pretend to be our friends, all the while beating us down.

True friends will stand beside us and make sure we don't get too beaten up. It's not the job of a friend to intervene in life's whippings–that would put too much burden on others as our lives are our responsibility. A good friend is always a steady hand holding us up as life challenges our balance.

Gorilla's graduation party is a testament to how much a true friendship can endure. When we find friends who will hold us up, we need to make sure we're there to hold them up as well and that we keep them around. Often, these are the friends with the most positive influespire on our lives. We need GODs around us if we want to be GODs ourselves.

Insane Drinking Wisdom
EMBARRASSING CLOSE FRIENDS WHILE DRUNK IS OK, AS LONG AS WE ALWAYS HAVE THEIR BACK AND ARE OK WITH BEING MADE FUN OF IN RETURN!

With true friends, we can cross lines we wouldn't with others. We can experience the embarrassments and failures with a friend and still stand beside them. Our family, who is meant to be there through it all, will sometimes abandon us if we do something wrong or a secret comes out which goes against the family values, but a true friend never will. Friends are often closer than cousins and more valuable than gold. But how exactly do we form and maintain these true friendships?

To answer that, we have to start at the beginning–the first benefit of making friends. When we're young, our initial pack consists of just our family. In the world of only family, our life is similar to other family members, but a friend introduces us to a new world.

Think back to the first dinner at a friend's house. When we eat at a friend's for the first time, it feels like entering a different world. Even if we live on the same street, eat the same cuisine, and share the same culture and religion, no two homes are alike. There are small differences from how the food is prepared, to conversation topics at dinner, to how families interact. Once we've been over to a friend's house a couple of times, we can even walk into their house blindfolded and know whose house it is from the smell of it.

All friends–but especially our first ones–show us the nuances that make us different and alike. They teach us what love can look like outside of a family unit and how cyclical life can truly be.

I was lucky to grow up on a street where there were twenty kids around the same age. The proximity meant we played together almost every day. Whenever I was bored, I could run onto the streets and shout, "Does anyone want to play?" Most likely, someone would emerge from their house, eager for an adventure, and we would run around the neighborhood together. Normally, I wouldn't come home until I'd spent hours in the sun, exhausted by running and playing so much, and had sweat dripping down my face.

Within a group of twenty, there are always some people we're closer to than others. For me, there were two kids I was especially close with in primary school. My relationships with these twenty shifted when I reached high school. By university, I stopped speaking to almost all of them on a regular basis. Forty years later, I'm still close to four and will occasionally reach out to five others. I don't know anything about the others' lives, but no matter if I'm still close to these friends or not, they played a pivotal role in influespiring me to become who I am today.

If we want friends, we have to put intentional effort into forming these bonds. We can't just expect friends to come to us, as we might die alone while waiting for them to arrive. Some ways we can put intentional effort into making friends include:

- Go to places we love on our own and starting conversations with others who are there. Someone who loves a bookstore could go there and start up a conversation with another shopper.
- Attend events or in-person clubs around our interests. If someone likes to cook, they could join a cooking club while a volleyball fan could join a community volleyball team.
- Start conversations in public instead of always being on our phones
- We can talk to people in workout classes, at the cafe, at work–even on public transport.
- Join social media groups, go on Meetup.com, or use other digital sources to make friends who live in our area and share some of our interests.
- Invite interesting acquaintances out for lunch or to grab a coffee. We're all afraid to be the first to extend the invite, but we're grateful when someone else does.

All of these might feel uncomfortable, as it is not easy to be the one who makes the first step toward a stranger. But the worst that will most likely happen is receiving a puzzled stare back as the target of our outreach slowly walks away from us. This way we would know it was not meant to be, rather than wonder about it later, as we move on to the next person. And as with everything, the more we do it, the easier it gets.

Be the person who reaches out 🤍

As we generate friendship bonds through shared experiences–intentional or unintentional–we need to figure out if they are a true friend, aka if we can trust them. If someone passes a trust test we subconsciously give them, they can become a friend. If they fail, the trust needed to be true friends is lost.

An example is hearing a rumor around the class about us loving Sally after we mentioned liking her to an elementary school classmate the day before. The trust is broken and difficult to recover.

The more times a friend proves we can trust them or that they're kind to us, the deeper the friendship becomes. But when they break our trust or say something emotionally abusive, the friendship is more likely to fall apart 💔

Just like with every human relationship, friends get jealous or aren't happy over something that happened. As life goes on and we change as individuals, we start shifting between who we see as friends and who we don't. If our habits, values, and goals change, often our perception of current friendships and what we look for in new friends changes as well.

Friendships, like anything else in life, are cyclical. Many friends come into our lives. Some stay and some fall away. Sometimes they fall away slowly, other times it ends in a bad argument which feels as painful–if not more painful than–a breakup. And some return stronger than ever. Even our idea of a friend can change with age as well.

In my life, one of the best examples of this is how my group of 20 friends changed throughout my life. Even the 20 people I was closest to differed from life stage to life stage. Those changes were gift s in disguise–they allowed me to weed out (consciously or unconsciously) one-sided friendships and invest in ones which were mutually beneficial.

Due to insecurities or naivety, we've all experienced a one-sided friendship at one point or another. A friendship must be a give and take. When someone is only sucking energy from us and taking more than they give, they become an energy vampire. Vampires serve a role in cheesy teenage movies, in real life, they can impact how we view ourselves in the world. They feed off our dreams, eating them away.

Signs of energy vampires include:

- They're always involved in drama
- We feel drained after hanging out with them
- They make our problems feel smaller and their problems feel bigger
- They don't take accountability for their actions
- They always one-up us or downplay our wins

This is, of course, not an exhaustive list of signs, but it gives us a good idea of who they are–and even how to recognize when we are acting as an energy vampire so that we can heal within and have better interactions with others.

As we get older, we become better at spotting these energy vampires and cutting off connection with them—and sometimes getting them access to the mental health resources they need to heal. Because of this, we're constantly refining our criteria of who can be considered a friend and who cannot.

We choose our friends and they choose us. But it's not a one and done choice. For a friend to become a lifelong one, we need to decide to put in an effort to maintain that friendship—over and over again. This maintenance can get harder as lives get busier, distance grows, and we forge our own path, but it's also crucial.

There is, of course, one exception to this cycle. When a friendship gets very good, we might not speak to someone for a couple of years, but the next time we speak to them, it feels like we just spoke to them yesterday. These are the best kind of friends. But before that point—and even after—some maintenance is needed, like weeding a garden and watering plants to make sure they keep growing.

Friendships, like anything good in life, must be maintained.

I once had a conversation with a friend who complained that no one ever called him. I recommended he called up a couple of friends first. He responded, "Yeah, but why should I be the one to call first?"

This sort of mindset isn't just dangerous to our agency, it's also a great friendship killer. Making friends and maintaining friends is something which requires effort, a truth we often forget.

We always have to be intentional about our friendships. Our friendships, like our loves, should be selfless–it shouldn't be all about ourselves and we shouldn't feel resentful if we feel we have to put in more effort, as long as we're doing it for the good of our friends, not ourselves. Some actions to maintain friendships include:

- Having a network tracker for our social life that gives us a nudge if we haven't reached out to someone every so often. Network trackers don't have to be for just professional relationships!
- Texting someone when we see something that reminds us of them.
- When dreaming of someone, tell them the next day, regardless of who they are.
- Not being afraid to reach out and ask someone to catch up every once in a while.
- Ask people how they are–and genuinely care about the answer.

Of course, even if we maintain friendships, some will outlast others. These are the people we should hold on to for life–the ones we are the most grateful for and those we will sacrifice the most for, outside of our families. When we have true friends, we can expect them to be there for us, even on a humiliating night out after graduation.

FIRST, *CONSIDER FRIENDSHIPS* OF THE PAST AND PRESENT AND WRITE DOWN OTHERS' QUALITIES THAT HAVE *ENHANCED LIFE* AND WHICH QUALITIES MADE *LIFE WORSE*.

SECOND, THINK ABOUT HOW THE *BAD QUALITIES* CAN BE AVOIDED AND THE *GOOD ONES* INTEGRATED INTO *FRIENDSHIPS*, BOTH NEW AND OLD.

THEN, FOCUS ON THE *GOOD QUALITIES* LIST AND COME UP WITH A COUPLE OF WAYS TO MAKE NEW FRIENDS BY SEEKING OUT *THESE QUALITIES IN PEOPLE*.

FINALLY, TRY TO *IMPROVE FRIENDSHIP MAINTENANCE* BY EMBRACING THESE *GOOD QUALITIES* DAILY.

THIS IS A *TOUGHER EXERCISE* COMPARED TO PREVIOUS ONES, BUT I DID SAY THAT GOOD FRIENDSHIPS *REQUIRE EFFORT* ☺

While friends can have a positive influespire on our life, the impact of our family can make us or break us. Let's gear up to analyze our crazy families!

Chapter 6:
We Binge Family

This is the end, my friends. The end of my world as I knew it 😳

In July 2018, my grandad turned ninety. The whole family on my
mother's side was gathering in our hometown in Veneto. The family
spent an entire year organizing this event and my wife, kids, and I were
kicking off our summer holidays with this celebration. My family was
scheduled to fly to Venice on Friday, July 20th, while I was going to drive
our Hyundai I-20 for twelve hundred kilometers across Europe.
That's not exactly a nice, relaxing drive, but we needed the car in Italy
since we were going on vacation to Croatia after. I had done the trip a
few times before, sometimes in a single day–17 hours of driving in a 24
hour period takes a toll. Instead of repeating that dreadful experience,
I took off late on Thursday in a car fully packed for the holidays.

Both my brothers were traveling back home as well. We usually only see each other once a year, if we are lucky, and all three of us are together even less often because we all live in different countries. Since we were all going back, we seized the opportunity to celebrate. Our reunion would take the form of a few drinks once we all arrived in Italy.

That Friday, I didn't hit snooze on my alarm once–a serious feat. I scarfed breakfast down in one minute, threw on the shirt from the day before, and brushed my teeth. I was on the road by eight, thrumming my hands against the steering wheel, excited to see my brothers again.

11 hours later, I arrived at my mother-in-law's house, my wife and children were already there and, after unloading most of the luggage, we had dinner–pizza of course. We are Italian after all!

If any other pizza lovers are curious, we had a pepperoni and mushroom pizza, my favorite. I gobbled my food down and left within an hour to drive to my grandparents, where I was going to stay for the weekend. I kissed my wife goodbye and agreed to meet the next morning at my grandparents' house. Little did I know what the next morning had in store for me 😟

My mom, my grandma and my grandpa were over the moon when I arrived. The excitement of having an adult child home never diminishes, even if said child recently visited. I gave a big hug to my grandad who had turned ninety the day before. An amazing milestone for him as he continues to march on to his 120 years goal.

After a quick shower and a change of clothes, I darted to the door saying to not wait up for me. My brothers and I had plans that night. Even though we had agreed to a couple of light drinks, I expected to drink quite heavily that evening.

I left my car parked behind the church and walked to the osteria. I was tired after a full day of driving and rushing, but thrilled to see my brothers and spend a proper night out drinking.

As I have abundantly written about so far, I have spent many of my nights drinking–all of them including more drinks than intended. Despite all the misadventures, it has always been a pleasure to spend time with friends. After I moved to the Netherlands, I cut back on my drinking and the time spent with friends scaled back (unintentionally) too.

In my early forties, nights out with friends became even rarer. I loved spending time with my people, carefree and enjoying each others' presence and the alcohol. I had so many nights like these throughout my teens and twenties and so few after. After the Netherlands move, I missed my family and friends, but did not miss one aspect of living in a tight-knit community: family drama verging on trauma.

Of the three groups we've discussed in this influespire, family is the most important. Unlike friendship and work, it's the one we are born into and the one which teaches us the most about the world. Our families can influence in a variety of ways, some good, some bad.

For example, our families can influence:

- How we love others
- How we parent our children
- How we parent ourselves
- What we chose to do as a career
- What we value in life
- Our relationship with money
- Our relationship with friends
- How we enter romantic relationships
- If we prioritize work over family or family over work
- How confident we feel in our own capabilities

The list could go on and on. When our family life is bad growing up, it often has negative impacts on us, even as adults. Yet even good families can sometimes cause us to feel minor traumas (not Trauma with a capital T which is diagnosable, but small, painful memories that have shaped us into who we are today).

I was fortunate enough to grow up with two parents and an extended family who loved me, though in their own ways.

Since my dad left our family when we were young, he loved us from afar. When I did see him, he was constantly judging others, including myself and my younger brothers. Though even through the judgment and distance, I could feel his love. He wanted what was best for his children, but expressed it in the wrong way (judgment and criticism to make us all better), which is something many of us can relate to.

My mom's love and how she approached the family image were different. She smothered my brothers and I. If dad's love was distant, nothing could be closer—and at times suffocating—than my mom's adoration for her sons. While my dad preferred to judge others, my mom cared about what others thought and wanted us to go to church all the time. She used to dress my brother and I exactly the same, which is sometimes normal for twins, but not really for two kids who are eighteen months apart, because she thought it made us look better as a family.

As one might imagine, this polarity between how my mom and dad loved created some tension growing up. And I'm sure I'm not the only one who felt this way.

As humans, we are all flawed. It's in our nature to feel insecure, to get distant or too close, to hurt others and be hurt in return. These flaws are perhaps best expressed in our familial relationships. While our parents love us, they also bring their flaws along with that love. In fact, there are two truths to living life as a human:

- We will make mistakes. This is inevitable.
- Our love has flaws because none of us are perfect.

Even the best, most well intentioned parents will make mistakes in raising their children because as humans, it's impossible to do anything flawlessly. What helps, of course, is parents who are actively trying to understand their own trauma, how it manifests in relationships with their kids, and how to heal it. For children to understand how their parents negatively affected them, distance helps.

That's part of why I went to the US for a year of high school. My parents had split just before I turned thirteen and their peculiar ways of loving us simply got worse. So three years later, I decided to try to understand myself apart from my family by going to America. 10 years after that, my wife and I moved to the UK in order to be able to start our own family.

Leaving our families behind was good for us. Families, even when healthy, can be a constraint. They can expect us to take over a family business instead of following our passions and dreams or show up weekly at a religious institution for a faith we don't believe in. They always have an opinion about our lives, even if they haven't experienced anything similar to what we are going through. Distance from those uninformed, but loving opinions can often be a good thing. It leaves spaces for us to find ourselves.

Because we were thousands of kilometers away from our families and only saw our families on holidays, we found a way to pursue our dream to build our own family and life. Even if we don't decide to make a physical move, it's always best to analyze our interactions with our family and decide how much mental space is needed.

Self Discovery Exercise

THINK OF SOME TIMES FAMILY INFLUENCED ACTIONS. JOT THEM DOWN AND WRITE A POSITIVE OR NEGATIVE SIGN NEXT TO EACH.

FROM THERE, CONSIDER IF FAMILY HAS A NET-POSITIVE OR NET-NEGATIVE IMPACT AND HOW TO CHANGE FAMILIAL RELATIONSHIPS IF IT IS NET-NEGATIVE.

Many of the societal preferences from the third influespire level are passed down through the family. While religious beliefs are decided by a community, it's often family who forces us to follow without questioning.

Families often believe they own their children, which isn't completely surprising since in the past, parents would sell their children. Or, in the case of daughters, they would incentivize someone to take a woman away from her family by giving a dowry to the husband.

In families, it's easy to feel like we have to do something, not that we want to do something. Families can make us forget that we are GODs and renounce our dreams to follow theirs.

This is perhaps best seen in dynasties where nepotism runs rampant. Nepotism is the art of destroying businesses and legacies by passing along leadership roles to unqualified or unwilling relatives instead of qualified and determined people outside the family.

In my more than fifteen years in business, I always said I would never hire my family members because none of them had the skill set for the roles I had to fill.

Nepotism in Italy is more common than in other places. In fact, the English term nepotism comes from the Italian term "nepotismo"–aka the practice of giving positions to relatives. The term comes from the middle ages, when popes gave coveted positions to their children (even though they weren't supposed to have children). While the church no longer practices nepotism, it has become an all-too-recognizable cultural trait, because in time, we all end up doing what we see. People shouldn't hire family members under most circumstances, though they often do.

Today, it's not uncommon for police officers or military personnel to push family members to join the force or for parents to pass their businesses on to their children in Italy. This is especially the case with unfit family members who can't find any other jobs.

Other cultures have been known to kill the black sheep of the family, but in Italy, these members sometimes are given executive roles in the family business... ideally with minimal responsibilities so they don't impact the bottom line.

In cultures like Italy, the family plays an important role and its strength can ruin family members and work dynamics. Like alcohol, family power is intoxicating and hard to quit. It blurs our judgment and makes us believe we're creating a good situation for ourselves and those around us.

Families influence us by constantly telling us what to do, but they also inspire us by simply being together, through the love and care they provide us with. As already mentioned, **they have the power to make or break us.**

But let's go back to the osteria, which for those who didn't grow up in Italy, is a traditional Italian bar (similar to a dive bar in the US or UK). As I mentioned, it had been a while since I'd been able to fully let myself go and enjoy the impacts of alcohol. We kept drinking and drinking, bringing back the familiar feeling of the weekends in Villach.

Even though I was tired from the eleven hour drive across Europe, my brothers wanted to go to another bar. As we know, I never say no to another drink! We got to this second bar already tipsy and had another beer. After that beer, we were drunk enough to believe that cocktails were a good idea. We transitioned to cocktails and kept drinking until I was drunk enough to bargain with the bartender. "I'll give a ten euros tip for more liquor," I begged the bartender.

Insane Drinking Wisdom
ALWAYS BRIBE BARTENDERS WITH BIGGER TIPS WHEN TOO DRUNK TO BE SERVED.

By closing time, we'd been unsuccessful at convincing a bartender to give us extra alcohol in our cocktails but we did manage to get hammered. My brothers caught a taxi back to their place. I was within walking distance of my grandparents' house so I decided to walk instead. The walk–a half mile–had been one I'd done time and time again since childhood. At this point, I felt my teeth entirely large 😬

I was completely drunk, walking alone up a hill at 2am. The street had a sidewalk and even though I tried my best to stay on it, I found myself shifting over to the middle of the street. When I realized I had veered into the street, I would walk back over to the sidewalk. Luckily no one was driving by, and even luckier, no one was filming me. The cycle between veering onto the street and sidewalk continued until I got to my grandparent's house.

When I got to the house, it was pitch black. I decided to slide along the wall in the dark instead of turning on any lights. My main goal was not to disturb anyone, yet my throat ached for water by the time I got to the kitchen. I turned on the kitchen light and grabbed some water–a good refresher before tackling my grandparent's big, spiral staircase. When I tried to conquer the stairs, I fell to my knees. I crawled, pulling myself by the rail, until I got to the floor where my childhood bedroom was.

When I got to that floor, I went to the bathroom. Luckily, Italian bathrooms have bidets which are easier to throw up in than toilets because they are closer to the ground. I would throw up and then turn on the water–usually used to wash shit off one's ass–and I would rinse puke off my face. I kept throwing up, rinsing, and repeating for a couple of hours until I heard a knock, knock, knock.

"Aureo, Aureo," a voice called up.

As I opened my eyes, bright light blinded me and I blinked them closed, headache pulsing. Eventually, I managed to look at my phone on the floor. It was 7:30am. The sunlight coming into the bathroom illuminated everything–the puke crusted on my mouth, the mushrooms and pepperoni from the night before were in the bidet, and my clothes were disheveled from the night before. My head laid on the bathroom rug, a pillow I would not recommend.

When I opened the door, my grandfather exclaimed through his tears, "Thank god, we thought we would have to climb through the window." He had woken up in the middle of the night to go to the bathroom and found the door locked. He thought I had gone to the restroom at the same time as him and went to the other bathroom in the house.

At 7am, the door was still locked. Panicked, he grabbed my mom and they knocked on the door for over a half hour with no answer from the other side. By the time I'd opened the door, my grandad had thought of the worse case scenario so the reality didn't seem as bad.

To my mom, it wasn't as great. She complained, "Aureo, look at this bathroom."

It was in quite the state. The toilet paper was flung on the ground. Puke lined the bidet and dripped onto the ground–and onto my face. I must have tugged a towel down at some point because it was half laying on me, half catching a conditioner dripping. The bottle must have leaked at some point throughout the night.

But the bathroom didn't matter. All I focused on was my grandad and how the pain of potentially losing his first grandchild could have caused a ninety-year-old to have a heart attack or stroke. I had been more drunk than even an average Villach night, so I was relieved just to be alive and for my family to be alive, even though I was far from well-rested.

My mom complained more until I reassured them it wouldn't happen again. My grandad twisted the reality to what he wished it to be. "Oh he must have passed out because he was tired," he reassured my mom.

But moms always know what's going on. I could tell from her glare that she knew I had been well beyond drunk the night before.

After we cleaned up the bathroom, I showered and went to sleep for a couple of hours before the doorbell rang. I came downstairs and saw my wife in the kitchen. My wife gave me a look I recognized: the disappointment she wore whenever I drank that much.

"I already told her everything," my mom taunted.

At the time, we'd already been together for over 20 years and throughout our marriage, I heavily drank. My wife was used to stuff like this, but it didn't make it any easier for her to cope with it. The drunken mistakes grew fewer and fewer the older I got, but that made the fallbacks into drinking more painful. For each day I went without drinking, my wife's hope that I had finally kicked the habit for good rose–and fell harder when I drank again.

Seeing a loved one slip back into bad habits is never easy, especially if we think they quit for good.

As planned, we went to tour my mom's new house. While my wife, mom, and kids went to see the inside, I threw up in the garden. We were supposed to go to lunch at my mother in law's house after, but I opted out, choosing the bed over family conversations. Even the thought of food made me nauseous.

The next day, we had the celebration for my grandad's birthday. The whole family showed up to celebrate and during that day, I didn't touch any alcohol.

Having an entire family in one place is powerful, but celebrating the 90 years of my grandfather's life and time in our family supercharged community feeling that I got from my family. I grew up privileged since I lived in a family where it didn't matter what would happen, someone would always be there for me.

When our family loves us, it's a powerful safety net and reassurance. (It's also why it's important to find friends and others who give us this family-feeling, especially if one's original family doesn't act much as a family.)

As a kid, I grew up in a loving environment (though there were fights and clashes, some mentioned in this chapter 🙈). I always had grandparents' houses to go to, family events to look forward to, and people who accepted me as I was.

No one's family is perfect. Mine, for example, initiated me to drinking. I first started drinking at my grandparents' house and ultimately stopped there too, completing a 35 year-long cycle. But they are there for us no matter what and are usually our first exposure to love.

The community-feeling and love-spreading are what we should take away from our family—we should ask ourselves how we can better serve those around us to create the love of a family anywhere we go. The selfless love my grandparents fed me throughout my childhood made me who I am today.

We've all had arguments with family members or disagreed with their actions, but what matters is the love and care that they show us. When we prioritize bringing positive energy to our families, the moments where we come together are far more powerful than the disagreements. In the case of my grandparents, they had been channeling positive energy into the family throughout their lives and they showed us all how we could give that energy back to our family and teach future generations to do the same.

At my grandad's birthday, we experienced what we had built: a supportive familial community. That day made me reflect on my role within the community and what I could do to provide support to my family. This spurred me to create a life change which transformed my influespire on those around me. I didn't want to scare loved ones with thoughts that I could die of an alcohol overdose. Instead, I wanted to inspire them and make them feel loved and cared for. To this day, I haven't drunk once. I had already drunk my lifetime quota of alcohol by the age of 42 anyways.

Now, I no longer feel the need to drink. Even in social settings where everyone is drinking, the pressure to drink has slipped away and I instead opt for a soda or water.

This is how our family can influespire us to do better. Whether it's through almost giving a grandad a heart attack or being unable to handle the disappointment of a romantic partner, protecting our family can change our actions for the better.

Self Discovery Exercise

HOW CAN OUR FAMILIES INFLUENCE US TO DO BETTER AND HOLD US ACCOUNTABLE?

When we think about our families, we should focus on the best they have given us. We can look for those traits in friends and/or use those traits as guiding principles in our professional careers. Our families, jobs, and friends can influespire us to achieve our dreams and teach us valuable lessons if we focus on the positive impact of our pack.

But it's not enough just to look at the positives of our pack. We have to actively change our lives for the better and this has to come from the first influespire level: the self. Next, we'll dive into how we as individuals can embrace what we are. And what we are is GODs and creators of our own destiny.

Chapter 7:
A Glorious Drink

And so it begins: the journey into the self. So far, we've examined the two more "comfortable" (comfort being relative) influespire levels: our society and our pack. Now it's time for that thing we never want to examine, but we need to in order to thrive: the self.

Our own internal dialogue and way of processing the world count for much more than we think. Without the self, there would be no pack or society to experience. But its importance doesn't make it any easier to face, especially when it comes to the parts of ourselves we'd rather keep hidden. Yeah. We're talking about the Freudian skeletons in the closet. But don't worry–we (probably) won't dig out any skeletons in this chapter. We'll save that for later ☺

Let's start nice and easy with knowledge. Simply put, knowledge is power. We've all heard this so many times, but we rarely stop and think about what this means for our own lives. Before we think about that, let's take a moment to get drunk on knowledge. Because what haven't I gotten drunk on?

While attaining knowledge is something I strive for today, I didn't always have this love affair with learning new ideas and ways of being. For a large part of my life, I was a pretty bad student–both in school and in the "school of life."

After I graduated high school, I sat down and had "the talk" so many of us have at 18 with our parents–not the sex talk for any dirty minds out there (that should actually happen much earlier). The one where our parents ask what we want to study at university and we throw out a crazy, idealistic idea for our career.

For me, this was being an astronomer or philosopher. I wanted to take big concepts–whether outer space or my internal thoughts–and share them with the world. When I told my mom, she frowned and said, "That's great, sweetie, but that won't put food on the table."

There's a moment in all our lives when the messaging of society goes from: we can be anything we want when we grow up to how much does that job pay? It's kinda a sucky moment and it had caught up to me. The expectations–from both the third and second influespire levels–had infiltrated my psyche. How was I going to pay my bills and put food on the table by looking at stars all day?

So I chose a major which didn't excite me but would excite my bank account: engineering. I was going to be an engineer, never mind that I'd barely passed high school physics and math. Or that the career bored me to death. In my first semester at university, I took chemistry and calculus... and failed both.

So I did what any 19 year-old boy faced with failure would do: I ran away and joined the army. While my time in the army taught me about discipline and hard work, it also showed me that it wasn't the path for me. (We need to remember to be grateful for the paths we head down which show us who we don't want to be.)

I wanted to graduate from university. Knowledge should have played a bigger role in my life and even with the failed first semester, I decided to go back to studying. I asked around to see what my friends were studying–and what the wealthiest people I knew did for a living.

That's when I came across a career which would let me get that cash money: economics. Even though both degrees started with an E, I vowed this time would be different. No running away. No failed classes. No quitting to join the army. Just me, the books, and studying (and nights out at the Irish pub, of course).

One of my first classes in the sequel of university was economics 101. For the final (oral) exam, we had to answer three questions. Students who answered two correctly would pass.

Not only was this exam an oral one, it was much longer than the normal two-hour, teeth grinding, nerve-wracking exams we're used to. Instead of sitting, watching the clock ticking and praying to complete all the questions before the timer beeped in the front of the lecture hall, we sat in an exam room for three days. We would watch as student after student was called to the professor. They'd answer three questions, get their score, and then leave. Students passed or failed right on the spot, in front of everyone. We never knew when our name was going to be called, adding an element of surprise. I always had the feeling Italian universities were more about teaching to deal with bizarre procedures and unnecessary stress more than the actual topic of study.

Now, here's the annoyingly frustrating thing about me: I always put in the minimum amount of effort possible. While this has served me well throughout my career (work smarter, not harder), an anxiety lingered within me when I returned to school that semester. Somewhere in the back of my mind was the taunting thought, "I'm going to fail again." Somehow, that thought didn't scare me enough because I didn't really study for this first exam.

But luck was on my side. I was one of the last five people out of 400 students to go. When the professor called my name for my oral exam, the room was deserted. Almost all students were already on their ski vacations, enjoying the winter wonderland instead of the fluorescent light of an academic hall.

The professor was already tired from administering 45 other oral exams that day, so the bar was low, empty, and in my favor. I got a 21/30 on the exam. 18 was the necessary number to pass and I barely surpassed it–but it was my first time passing a university exam!

My friends waited for me outside, eager to hear the results. A giddy smile spread across my face and they didn't even have to ask me if we were celebrating or mourning my academic career. They cheered and my best friend (remember Gorilla?) patted me on the back.

For our plans, it didn't matter if I passed or failed because we would have gone to the same place: the Irish pub for beers. While we did this more nights during university than I care to admit, this night was different–more to celebrate equals more drinking!

Insane Drinking Wisdom

**WHETHER TRIUMPHANT OR BEATEN,
DRINKING IS ALWAYS A GOOD IDEA.**

A night at the Irish pub in celebration instead of drinking one's sorrows is a lot nicer too.

The night started with three beers, then four, then five. Halfway through the night, I'd had almost a gallon of beer with no intention of stopping. The feeling of success filled me, making me lighter than anyone else, and the alcohol made me float higher. I was the happiest person around and the day was one of my happiest days drinking.

On our way from the Irish bar to the next, we came across a friend of a friend, a girl I'd never seen before. I shouted, "I passed my first exam! I passed my first exam!" Like a brutish, Nordic thunder god, I smashed my beer glass on the street (remember that scene from the Marvel universe?).

This is something I would never do today–nor recommend for anyone else to do–but I was so hyped on passing my exam and so drunk on the beer that it seemed like the right decision at the time.

While my friends and I had plenty of nights celebrating good exam scores at that pub, this one stands out because it was such a pivotal moment. It was the moment I realized knowledge is power–not only because a college degree would get me a better job, but because it changed me. The knowledge I learned in my economics 101 class didn't just improve my understanding of that field; it also increased my confidence and showed me that I could pass a university-level exam.

So often the word knowledge brings about images of textbooks, university halls, and final exams. We let letter grades handed out by someone else determine how much knowledge we have and school teaches us to use those letter grades to determine our identity: the jock who could care less about school, the straight-A student who barely tries, the one who does anything for the grade, including pulling all nighters.

But knowledge isn't just what we're taught in school–and it's dangerous to let others determine what it means to us. When others tell us what is and isn't "knowledge" they determine what's important, not us. We allow them to shape our dreams. And everyone should always determine what matters to them and what their dreams are.

Let's say there's a college student named Jeb who really loves the science of dating. Jeb wants to create an app that helps LGBTQ+ members find better potential matches. When Jeb tells the idea to a professor, the professor laughs and tells him to focus on knowledge that matters, such as cybersecurity. Jeb enrolls in extra cybersecurity courses, leaving no free time to create the app. The knowledge which could help thousands find long-term relationships is lost because someone else told Jeb what is and isn't worth studying and understanding. Jeb's dream is gone. Maybe forever, maybe not. With luck, many others will have this dream and might even collaborate with Jeb to pursue it again.

Now, ironically, let me present a different idea of what knowledge could be. If this conception doesn't resonate with someone, they should find a different one. Again, we shouldn't let anyone control what knowledge means to us personally. This definition is simply food for thought.

Knowledge often starts with one individual and ripples through all three influespire levels. Thanks to the push from all three levels, a dream can become something useful instead of an abstract concept. Check out these examples:

Dream: The Internet

Individually: While it's hard to come up with one individual who created the internet, let's focus on the earliest individual to conceptualize the idea: Nikolas Tesla. Tesla tried to create the world's first wireless communication system in the early 1900s.

Our Pack: After Tesla failed, some fellow scientists reviewed his work and kept trying to create the internet. Eventually, they got funding from the US Department of Defense for the project.

Our Society: Because Nikolas Tesla toyed with the idea, the US Department of Defense could create a wireless communication system almost 100 years later and then open it up for the public to use in the 1990s.

Dream: Smallpox Vaccine Distribution

Individually: Ladies from aristocratic courts read books on how if someone was inoculated with a small bit of the smallpox virus, they would be immune to it.

Our Pack: These women pushed for the vaccine to be available at royal courts around Europe, from Russia to Great Britain. Since these women had social capital, aka came from noble families, the ideas caught on faster than when scientists themselves would try to advocate for this new vaccine technique.

Our Society: Smallpox became widely treatable because smallpox vaccinations were given out to much of the European world (and later the entire world).

Dream: Beatlemania

<u>Individually</u>: Beatlemania is not a dream per se, but boy, was it a collection of so many dreams becoming reality. And it started with John Lennon loving to play music and wanting to start a band, slowly playing with more and more musicians until the Beatles formed.

<u>Our Pack</u>: Their first followers watched their performances in clubs in Liverpool and Hamburg, giving the band the chance to live on their music and continue creating.

<u>Our Society</u>: Eventually, their songs and views took over the youth around the world, pushing a counterculture revolution spanning from music to peace, from drugs to love.

Dream: Wikipedia

<u>Individually</u>: Jimmy Wales loved knowledge and had the dream of creating a repository for all knowledge in the world. He came up with the idea of Wikipedia.

<u>Our Pack</u>: The first users saw the potential of this new endeavor and started contributing for free to its creation. The power of community drew users together and allowed them to deliver knowledge worldwide.

<u>Our Society</u>: Today, Jimmy's dream is a reality and it is being used all over the world to share and learn. I use it daily and have used it plenty of times while working on this book (after checking any information with other sources, of course).

*Knowledge comes in many shapes and forms but it's something which improves our lives, whether it improves them on the third, second, or first influespire level–or on all three. In fact almost every piece of knowledge out there impacts all three levels. Societies, our packs, and ourselves wouldn't exist as they do today without the invention of the printing press, antibiotics, computers, and the list goes on (and on and on and on and... we get the idea).

While all four of these examples are of varying importance, they all demonstrate how knowledge can influespire our lives, our packs, and our societies. But they all started on one level: the individual–because we are GODs.

As individuals, there are a lot of ways we can gain knowledge. Beyond formal education, we can also gain knowledge from:

- Instinct: Our instincts and intuitions guide us when we're quiet and listen. This is similar to how a bird knows what to do and how to do it.
- Survival Knowledge: this is knowledge either we ourselves learned or society as a collective learned in order to survive. This includes how to build a fire, hunt food, etc.
- Adaptation Knowledge: this is similar to survival knowledge, but unlike survival knowledge, we would survive without this, just not thrive in our specific society. This can include learning about pop culture, watching a TV show to fit in at work, or watching TikTok tutorials to do makeup a certain way.

- Career Knowledge: knowledge that we learn on the job which helps us better do our jobs and assimilate to the current work culture. Does anyone else have to learn an insane amount of acronyms anytime they join a new company?
- Social Knowledge: lessons transferred from our friends, family, and acquaintances about what is and isn't acceptable in different social situations. This might include our perceptions of drinking and how much is acceptable to drink at different social events.
- Passion-based Knowledge: this is when we seek knowledge on our own simply for the passion of it. Usually, this knowledge isn't "useful" in our day to day lives. If we listen to a podcast on medicine or true crime for fun but don't work in those fields, that knowledge would fall into this category.

There are other types of knowledge out there too, and the boundaries between types of knowledge are blurred, but these are the ones that first came to my mind.

Self Discovery Exercise
WHICH WAYS OF ACQUIRING KNOWLEDGE ARE THE MOST IMPACTFUL/IMPORTANT? ARE THERE OTHER WAYS THAN THE ONES MENTIONED HERE?

Once we have obtained a piece of knowledge, our brains process it in a way unique to anyone else's processing methods. From there, our brains interpret what that knowledge means about the world around us–and about ourselves.

We could all receive the same piece of knowledge and interpret it in very different ways. Just look at Sartre and Camus, who both supported the idea that life has no real meaning. Sartre believed that because life had no meaning, people should add meaning to their existence by pursuing what they want to do. Camus, on the other hand, interpreted this knowledge as since life has no meaning, any action someone takes is pointless and futile. One piece of knowledge, two opposite interpretations and applications. Basically, it's not what we know, but how we use it.

Knowledge doesn't determine our future.
How we process knowledge and respond determines it.

Two people, Francis and Juana, are both laid off from their jobs as graphic designers at big companies. Francis processes this knowledge to mean he sucks as a designer and shouldn't have even gone for the career in the first place. He takes the first job that will hire him and decides he will never design anything again.

Juana, on the other hand, processes this knowledge as the company is going through a tough time. In fact, her country is currently in a recession and few people have the money to hire a full-time graphic designer. But companies still need stuff designed so they're turning to freelance designers. Juana files for a business and takes on her first freelancing client the next day. Within a year, she's having more fun than at her old job, plus she is making more money.

When it comes to knowledge, it's not just use it or lose it. It's use it wisely or unwisely. So how exactly do we learn to process knowledge in a healthy way? How can we make sure we use the knowledge around us correctly? Like all things in life, it's easier and harder than it seems 👻

First, we must accept that exposure to a new set of knowledge, especially at first, can feel overwhelming–and that's because it is! We've all been in a situation where we picked up a new hobby or side hustle, bright-eyed and ready to be a terrific dancer, influencer, or insert-other-identity-here. But then we stumble over our own two feet in our first dance class or our first Instagram reel gets less than ten views.

The results we want aren't coming AND we're still overwhelmed because there are a million and one things we need to learn–and we also don't know what we don't know or what things will bring about success. This is normal–healthy even. In fact, when we start learning a new subject, we learn 80% of the new subject early on and only about 5% each year after we start learning, which is why percentage wise, learning something new is overwhelming.

Before COVID, I had already been working from home so it was easier for me to adapt to COVID regulations than for those who were used to going into the office every day. I already knew 80% of the knowledge (predicted), not exact needed to be productive when working from home. Others had to learn that 80% while going through a global pandemic–and most likely felt much more overwhelmed and frustrated by this experience.

Whether we're going through a global pandemic or not, adjusting to a new way of living can be rough. And many of us quit when what we should do is celebrate all the new knowledge and persist. We should be drunk on knowledge, not drinks!

Once we get over the overwhelm phase, there's another truth in life we must tackle: labeling some knowledge or experiences as good or bad. There's no such thing as "bad knowledge." As I said earlier in this chapter, knowledge of what we don't want to do in life, such as my time in the military, can actually be useful in pointing us toward what we do want.

Any knowledge that brings us a new experience or way of seeing things will help us progress in the new realities coming our way. By moving around and absorbing as much knowledge as we can, **we become the best version of ourselves.**

And it's important to absorb the good and the bad. In fact, we remember bad experiences more than good ones. Since our brains are wired to remember bad experiences, we should try to resist that bias and not give them more weight than good ones. The bad experiences don't have to harm us if we see them as learning experiences, not obstacles.

When I was a junior manager, I lost over 200,000 euros with one mistake. Not a good feeling. At the time, the initial reaction was to sweep the experience under the rug. I wanted to make sure no one else knew about that loss, but that wasn't possible. My conscience wouldn't allow it. Instead, I learned a valuable lesson by shining as much light as possible on it and by taking accountability for my mistake–**life always feels better once we own up to our wrongs instead of avoiding them.**

In some ways, that experience was bad. But I could label it as good since I learned far more that day than on days when I did everything right at my job.

Once we've made peace with the overwhelm and learned from the bad experiences, it's time to tackle the third big lesson about knowledge: we're never done acquiring it.

We will never know enough in our lifetime. Everything we learn, we learn from somebody else. That's why it's so important to be with others and absorb as much as possible from others.

On the individual level, we use pieces of knowledge to build our future, but when we collaborate and bring our knowledge together, it builds our pack's and society's dreams as well. As a society, we generate a dream and we use knowledge to realize the dream. We must be able to work in a cumulative, synergetic way in order to build anything big– either on our own, as a pack or in society.

Any big societal achievements, from nuclear power plants to rockets, were due to people coming together and compiling knowledge. It wasn't due to new materials being found or a single ah-ha moment. Society likes us to believe one man or woman discovers something big in a breakthrough moment when really, each discovery is a collective of different people and different ah-ha moments.

Albert Einstein was one of the hundreds of scientists that contributed to the realization of nuclear power, and all of them built on the knowledge produced by all the thousands of people that came before them. The collective knowledge of all of these people led to the discovery of nuclear power. Thanks to that communal effort we devised the power to destroy the planet and now, as a community, we need to develop the maturity not to do it.

If we think of a laptop, everything that's in one today has existed on Earth since the days of the caveman. Why didn't Fred Flintstone invent the MacBook? The human knowledge wasn't there, even if the materials were. We had to learn new ways to put the materials together until we generated the computer. And the computer was born as the synthesis of some raw materials combined with knowledge from millions and millions of people: from the first that mastered fire, to the one that dug copper, on to whoever made plastic from oil, to pretty much all mathematicians, all the way up to Turing.

All inventions are because of knowledge AND collaboration based on knowledge. When we work together, we can learn and build more but working together means we must all do our own part. (Remember chapter 1? Moving a table is easier when done together than alone.)

"We" will always do better than "I" and "I"

Doing our part in the pursuit of knowledge looks like following the three rules above: **move through the overwhelm of learning something new, treat the bad experiences as lessons, and know that we'll never know it all.** Once we've grasped these truths, it's time to commit to being an (active) lifelong learner.

We're all lifelong learners, but we're not all active ones. Learning is inevitable throughout our lives–even if we try to avoid it at all costs. Life constantly pushes new lessons our way and gives us new obstacles to surmount. BUT we don't all play an active role in our learning. Many of us wander aimlessly around, not searching for new lessons and ways to push ourselves further.

An active lifelong learner isn't just showing up to the school of life, they're actively pursuing their interests. They make sure they are in the right classroom, do all the homework, and participate in classroom discussions. Aka they commit to their role as lifelong learners in small and large ways each day.

Some other ways I personally commit to my part in acquiring knowledge for humanity include:

- Pushing my comfort zone and the boundaries of what I think is possible.
- Taking time each day to notice my surroundings, instead of passing by them.
- Asking questions all the time, even when I think I know the answer.
- Learning something new every day. This doesn't have to be formal either. It could happen in the form of a conversation with a stranger or discovering a new band I like.
- Putting myself in new situations and listening to knowledge that strangers have that I don't yet have.
- Following what interests me–and not being afraid to close cycles and start something new whenever I get bored or feel a change is needed.

All these commitments have one thing in common: they require action from me. The pursuit of the *right* knowledge–and the application of it–demands we engage with it and utilize it in our lives and work.

Self Discovery Exercise

IN WHAT WAYS CAN WE ALL TAKE ACTION TO BE LIFELONG LEARNERS? LIST SOME MORE WAYS WE CAN GROW OUR OWN KNOWLEDGE–AND THUS SOCIETY'S KNOWLEDGE–ON A DAILY BASIS?

Ok, enough about acquiring knowledge. How can we take ownership not only over what we know, but over our entire lives?

Chapter 8:
Dry Way

The entire purpose of this book (which we're taking the scenic route to because the scenic route is more fun) is to learn how we can equip ourselves to be a positive influespire in our societies, our packs, and our individual lives. While it's important to analyze how the two broader influespire levels–our societies and our packs–influence and inspire us, the self influespire level is where we can empower ourselves to live the life we want for ourselves and those around us.

The first tool on the individual level was knowledge. When we know how to better process and seek out knowledge, we are more confident in our ability to grow and act from love.

The second tool is even messier, and one we don't often like to discuss: ownership. No matter what actions we take, we must take ownership of those actions and their consequences. However, something usually gets in the way of us taking ownership: BS 🤢

And yes, we could interpret that as an acronym for bullshit or we could interpret it as my new acronym for blaming and supposing. Both are equally applicable.

Blaming
We hardly ever take ownership of our actions, especially when the action was taken by a group we are part of (country, race, religion, company). In a group, we delegate most of that ownership (and blame!) to others. Two places where this is extremely prevalent are the army and religion. In the army, people take orders from above and push the responsibility onto someone else. In religions, we push responsibility onto a god.

We saw this in the society influespire level and by now we can probably reflect on some examples of how nations, religions, and in-groups blame others when things go wrong. Though they're never shy to take the responsibility when things go right!

Blaming others can normalize almost any action, from burning "witches" and scientists during the Inquisition to genocides organized by evil governments around the world. Plus, it makes the blaming party feel like they're not at fault.

Even the concept of the patriarchy makes it easy to normalize abuse against women. In this example, it shifts the blame onto the victim: a woman must have been "asking for it" if she's sexually assaulted. And if a guy's sexually assaulted, it must not exist at all because it falls outside the patriarchal norms.

These actions can happen and can be normalized because we can take on the group's identity in exchange for others taking on some of the blame. This is especially true in our internet-obsessed world where we are constantly grouping ourselves and others. Some of these groupings are silly, though they can still cause harm to ourselves and others:

- GenZ will always be phone obsessed so it's fine if my teenage son is always on Snapchat.
- I work in finance and make a lot of money, so I'm too busy to be considerate of others.
- Millennials are all alcoholics so it's ok if I keep drinking.
- I'm a Gemini, so it's impossible for me not to be two-faced and to gossip because that's how Geminis are.
- Boys will be boys, so who cares if he pulls girls' hair in class?
- I've always been someone who votes this way so obviously I'm a good person.
- They can't expect me to do that. It's below my pay grade.

Whenever we identify with a group, we have to be careful to see how that identification impacts our decisions and if we like the person we are becoming. If not, we need to take ownership back onto ourselves.

As some readers might have picked up on, this leads us back to the influespire levels of our packs and society–who we blame is often dictated by who our packs and societies, at large, blame. But in the end, we are the ones doing the blaming.

We blame because we fear the consequences. Taking responsibility is a messy, time-intensive process. It can lead to both internal and external pain. The external pain coming from how others "punish" us while internally, owning the blame means looking at our flaws and shortcomings head-on. Neither of these is comfortable, but dealing with the fallout from ourselves and others is part of owning life.

Supposing
The opposite side of the same coin is supposing. When we blame, we're delegating our bad actions or misfortunes to someone else. When we're supposing, we are making life choices based on how we think others will respond–and how they will hopefully reward us. Supposing drives us to make decisions based on what others think is right–or more so what we think others think is right.

It's a way of living rooted in external validation. When we suppose, we turn to the external world around us and ignore the goals which come from within. We fail to understand what we really want. Here are some examples to help illustrate what supposing looks like in our lives:

- Many of us strive for a college degree because we suppose that will make our family happy or make us rich.
- A husband plans a romantic date night watching the movie his wife loves and he hates, because he supposes it will lead to sex afterward.
- We put in extra hours at a job we hate because we suppose that will lead to our boss promoting us.
- A child might try to study hard for the spelling bee because they suppose winning it will make their parents proud.
- We vote for a politician, supposing they will fulfill their promise to lower taxes or emissions.

All of these could work out great, but I'm sure we can all imagine how these scenarios might turn out for the worst. The movie night turns into an argument over never having sex after the wife claims to have a headache. The college degree our parents wanted us to get leaves us unfulfilled, hating the job it leads us to. The extra hours at work often go unnoticed and the parent may miss the spelling bee altogether because a work thing came up.

When they turn out this way, we blame the other party for making us believe these would have worked out great. But who was the one supposing from the start?

So if we all know that supposing doesn't automatically lead to personal fulfillment or long lasting praise from others, why do we all do it?

The answer is twofold:

1. *It's easier than deciding for ourselves*: humans are lazy–we are always looking for the easiest way to do something and listening to others is easy-peasy. If we suppose a certain career path will win us the approval of our parents and community, it's easier to go to university for that career than to stop and consider what would make us feel warm and fuzzy instead. But the path with the least resistance only occasionally leads to the goal we have in mind, so we should focus more on the goal than on following our fears.
2. *We crave others' approval*: like it or not, we all have expectations and desired actions from others. The desired actions can take the form of verbal praise or something more tangible, like a raise or winning a new client. Strangely enough, it feels good to be recognized even for doing things we did not want to do because it's someone else caring for us.

As we can imagine, both motives can lead to disappointment in ourselves and others. Most people ignore what others do because they're too focused on their own lives–to them, we are side characters and they'll adjust to whatever decisions we make.

In our own lives, we are the main character and any action we take has a direct impact on our lives. When we take actions based on others' judgments, we–not them–live with the consequences.

Living life only by others' standards is a recipe for failure.

Along with regretting our own life choices, we are also more likely to be disappointed in others. When we suppose, we have a specific desired reaction we want from those around us. But others don't usually act in the way we want them to–and that can lead to disappointment when we have built up expectations around how they'll react.

The best approach is to do things without expecting anything in return. If we take action based on how others will respond, we'll end up disappointed more often than not.

Basically, it's BS to do things based on how we suppose others will react and to blame others when things go wrong. These aren't stops on the road to success. Both lead us down the easy road (an easy road full of BS and NOT the lives we want). Taking ownership of our actions–and their consequences–is harder, but leads to a lot less BS in our lives.

Eventually, we realize that pursuing our goals is the path with the least resistance.

Self Discovery Exercise
HOW DOES BS (BLAMING AND SUPPOSING) SHOW UP IN OUR LIVES? JOT DOWN SPECIFIC EXAMPLES AS WELL AS THE CONSEQUENCE OF BS.

While there are many consequences when we blame others for our actions or suppose we should take certain steps to make others happy, all those consequences boil down to one, drunken metaphor: we come to the wheel after having a few too many shots and try to drive our lives.

I've discussed the village where I grew up and as who grew up in a rural setting can relate to, all of us kids were stuck in the village until we got our driver's licenses. And getting a driver's license greatly increases one's chances of dying. Treviso, the province where I lived, used to have the highest number of deaths from drunk driving in Italy.

To make it worse, no one wore seat belts at the time because it made one look like a bad driver. A good driver doesn't need a seat belt, after all! Still waiting for the logic on that thought to hit me 🙍

In fact, I had never worn seat belts to the point that when I was in the USA, I was laughing at owners of cars that had the automatic seatbelts, the ones that buckle up as the driver closes the door and sits down.

None of these statistics or tragedies ever stopped us from getting behind the wheel after a night of drinking. When I was 19, I would drive to a bar, drink with friends, and then drive back afterward. My friend group grew so accustomed to driving after the bar, we had a DDD (designated drunk driver) instead of a DD (designated driver who doesn't drink during the night). In our friend group, we were all our own DDD. We would drive ourselves home and many of us would wake up the next morning, not even realizing we had driven, as if we came home on autopilot. It was like playing Russian Roulette with my life–and my friends' lives and the lives of others on the road who one of us could have crashed into.

As one can imagine, this was a dark period in my community and many lives were lost, including one of my friend's. One night, he was driving drunk on a windy road surrounded by trees. He wasn't wearing a seat belt and had his window down, enjoying the summer night breeze blowing against his face. He veered a bit off the road at the wrong time–when a tree was right next to him on the side of the road.
The car hit the tree and flipped on its left side. My friend bounced off his seat, through the driver's window, and ended up smashed under the car, half inside and half outside.

Emergency services found his corpse, bloodied and alone, in the middle of the road. What wasn't there was the potential of all his life could be. All the lives he could have changed, all the experiences he never had, the future love of his life, his future children, his future career successes, his impact on the world. None of it was there. In its place was a corpse and a death which could have been prevented.

Not that I took any action to prevent similar deaths in the future right away. Even after that day, I continued to drive drunk, though I did wear a seatbelt after that death. My drunk driving habit continued until I moved to the UK.

In the UK, there were more laws and severe punishments against drunk driving–plus, it was just not as culturally acceptable as in Italy. When I came over to the Netherlands, public transport was more readily available and it was even easier to not drive drunk than to do it.

Now, I look back and see how severe the consequences of my drunk driving habit were. My friend crashed into consequences head-on and was murdered. I could have been too, all because I let the herd around me take me down the wrong path. If I had said to my friends that I wasn't going to the bar one night because I didn't want to drive home drunk, my friends would have seen that as a weakness. 25 years ago, drunk driving was still normal.

Since taking ownership of my life and the lives of others–and surrounding myself with those who feel the same way–it would now be crazier to drink and drive than to reject an invitation to go to the bar.

When the Italian government finally started cracking down on this dangerous habit, many people complained and resisted the necessary change, as if they were being asked to sacrifice their life or firstborn child. Change is hard, even when it is for our own good.

(In)sane Drinking Wisdom
DD > DDD
ALWAYS HAVE A DESIGNATED DRIVER,
NOT A DESIGNATED DRUNK DRIVER.

Our actions have a huge impact on those around us and the trajectory of our lives. When we take any action, we need to ask ourselves:

- What are the consequences of this action for myself?
- What are the consequences of this action for those around me?
- Am I ready to face the consequences?
- If not, how can I remove myself from this situation?

Further, driving our lives drunk isn't going to get us to our big dreams–but to BS and danger. Big dreams require hard work and difficult choices. They require us to own the consequences of our actions, not blame others and live life according to their idea of success. The decisions we make control our lives and we decide if we come to the wheel drunk (aka make easy choices) or come to the wheel sober (aka make hard choices).

Hard decisions make for an easy life.
Easy decisions make for a hard life.

Even if an easy life is more desirable, we all know deep down why it's so hard to make the right decisions: they don't feel comfortable in the moment. Pressing snooze feels so much better at the time than putting on our gym clothes and heading to the gym. Spending the weekend online or drinking with friends will feel much more fun than sitting down to write that novel. Hard choices have trade-offs. There's always something we must give up:

- Working on the business on a Friday night instead of partying
- Traveling the world at the expense of the promotion and corner office
- Deciding to stand up to the office bully instead of laughing with everyone else when he makes fun of Gerald from marketing

But easier decisions have a trade-off too. We don't always see them because the consequences are in the future, not the present like with hard decisions. But often, the tradeoffs for easy decisions are much uglier:

- Party every Friday night and never start the business which will change lives
- Get that promotion at work, but never see the world beyond one country because there's not enough vacation time to travel
- Never stand up for Gerald, only to later learn the office bullying caused depression and wrecked his mental health

And every easy decision listed has some BS. It includes blaming others or supposing a certain action is "right" or will bring external validation from others. The BS stops us from owning our lives and making those hard decisions which lead to fulfillment.

We own our lives when we make difficult choices based on the circumstances around us instead of based on society's expectations or what others want us to do.

When I quit university after failing out of my engineering degree, it was a hard decision, especially since everyone wanted me to continue on with school. Instead, I reexamined what I wanted and took ownership over my action–and the outcomes–instead of doing what I thought everyone else wanted me to do.

We only have one life.
Whatever we choose to do or not to do in this life is what we get.

But how exactly can we take more ownership over our lives today? We can make big sweeping changes, such as quitting our jobs or asking out our crush. But taking ownership can also come from small choices too:

- Cutting out Netflix on weeknights
- Deciding to get a mocktail on a night out
- Signing up for a yoga class
- Exercising twice a week–instead of zero times like last week
- Eliminating work email from a personal phone to reclaim our free time
- Devoting three hours each Saturday to work on a business

Do what is right, not what is easy. If we do what is right over and over again (no matter how small the "right decision" seems), we'll live an easy life.

Self Discovery Exercise
WHAT ARE SOME HARD DECISIONS THAT MAKE FOR AN EASY LIFE?
HOW CAN WE TAKE OWNERSHIP OF THOSE HARD DECISIONS AND SURROUND OURSELVES WITH THOSE WHO DO THE SAME?

Now let's talk about the one consequence we can never avoid, but try to anyways: death.

Chapter 9:
Who Wants to Drink Forever?

Ok, but before we discuss death, can I share one of my best drinking stories? I promise it's a good one. It involves waking up naked in a hotel room in Brazil, a note slipped under the door to call my wife.

The year was 2014 and I was six months into my new job. The role required a ton of travel, including a trip to Brazil near the end of the year. Not only was this my second December out of Europe, it was my first Christmas season in a tropical climate. Holiday decor and Christmas trees in the warm city of Sao Paulo made the holiday take on an entirely different vibe.

Throughout the week, I spent long days in meetings, though there was one event I was looking forward to: the company Christmas party on Thursday. The plan for the event was no meals, only some snacks and lots of free drinks–my kind of party!

Around 5:30pm, I left the office to eat something before heading to the venue. Others were heading straight from the office but as someone used to European winter weather (think snow-covered Christmas markets), I had to head back to the hotel to change into more comfortable clothing than my work suit. Not wearing shorts and a shirt when it was so nice outside would have been a crime. I also treated myself to a steak and a glass of red wine at the steakhouse to ensure I had a full stomach to absorb the alcohol that would have been flowing through my body.

The party was in a pub with nightclub-like qualities. The CFO had booked the entire venue for this event. Most of the festivities were set up on the ground floor where there was a big bar and space to dance. The stairs led to a balcony area where we could look down on the dance floor and spend time chatting away from the craziness. As soon as I walked in, I indulged in an equally dangerous and delicious drink: caipirinha! Someone offered me a beer, but I declined because of an insane drinking wisdom.

Insane Drinking Wisdom
**TO *AVOID A HANGOVER*, DON'T MIX THE TYPES OF DRINKS (WINES, BEERS, LIQUORS).
IF WE DO HAVE TO MIX THEM,
ALWAYS *GO UP* IN *ALCOHOL STRENGTH*.**

Since caipirinha and beer were the only drinks available on the company tab and I had to follow my insane drinking wisdom, I opted to only drink caipirinhas. For those who haven't had this Brazilian drink before, it's a wolf in sheep's clothing. It tastes like jungle juice, but has the kick of tequila shots.

As the night progressed, I chatted with some friends from the office, the general manager gave out prizes, and I had one (or maybe a couple) more caipirinhas. The warm weather and fun atmosphere put me into a relaxed mood–most likely the cocktails added to the energy too.

Around 10pm, I decided it was about time to say goodbye to everyone. My flight back to the Netherlands left the next evening. As I headed toward the exit, a girl approached me. She wanted to meet me, the guy from headquarters, to learn more about the direction of the company. This girl was relatively new to the company, so like me, she didn't have many people to engage with at the party.

The room was already spinning and the flight the next day flashed before my eyes when she asked what I would like to drink. I should have replied, "nothing. I need to head out." Instead, I said, "we should get two caipirinhas."

After the conversation, all I had drank that night hit. I found my way onto the dance floor. Everyone was dancing, shouting, and singing. The atmosphere was alive and energizing. So, naturally, I decided to drink more.

The last memory from the night was ordering a final (🤪) drink. I was already on a slippery slope to drunkenness when I ordered that mojito. But everybody else was too and I didn't really care...

Until I woke up completely naked with a horrible headache in my hotel room the next morning. As soon as I got up, I headed into the bathroom to throw up. Only a single piece of my steak came up, so I must have thrown up the rest sometime the night before. Not sure when or where, though.

But throwing up the steak wasn't the only lost memory. I had no idea what happened after that mojito or how I ended up in my hotel room. Before turning on my phone to see if there was any digital evidence of last night, I noticed a slip of paper slid underneath the door.

I picked it up. The note was from the hotel desk. It said my wife had called concerned and I should call her as soon as possible. There was a string of missed messages and calls to my wife on my cell phone. I'd also called my boss from my previous job (who luckily didn't pick up) and my insurance company.

I called my wife back, who was rightfully angry. Apparently I'd called her cell and the home phone multiple times in the middle of the night, but hadn't left a message. She had no idea where I was, what I was doing, or if I was in danger. In truth, I didn't either.

Despite being naked, I still had my passport, phone, and wallet with me, which meant I had been able to avoid being mugged, robbed, stabbed, kidnapped, or killed while wandering around Sao Paulo for a couple of hours in the middle of the night black-out drunk. I feel like I almost deserve a prize 🏆

After calling the hotel desk for a late check out, I decided to take a nap. As I drifted off to sleep, I reminded myself I needed to show up to the Brazil office before I left. Not only did I have some work to wrap up, I had to figure out who had taken me home and if I'd done anything else embarrassing last night. Oh god. What if I had done something that made me lose my job or had put my life or the lives of others in danger?

Four hours and a shower later, my teeth finally felt smaller again. I mustered up the energy to shave, so I looked less drunk, and headed into the office. A chorus of greetings and laughter followed me into the office. Some people showed videos or photos they had taken of me from the night before. Luckily, none were too embarrassing, though my dance moves left something to desire. No one gave me anything too useful on what had happened last night, though people had snippets of a night which seemed fun, if only I could remember it.

The girl I'd talked to earlier in the night, after my first attempt to leave, did say she saw me leaving and asked if I wanted a ride. Apparently, I spluttered "No, thanks!" and turned away from her, walking drunkenly into the darkness. No one had any memories of me after that.

Luckily, I made it onto my plane and home to the Netherlands. When I got home, my wife handed the kids off to me and said they were my responsibility for the weekend. In truth, I deserved all her anger and my wife deserved a weekend to herself. Monday, when I went into the office, a friend asked if I had been drinking. Evidently, I still looked and sounded drunk on Monday from that Thursday night. Ironically, the hangover headache persisted too.

What I didn't have from that night were memories of what happened between dancing and waking up in my hotel bed. If I had met the wrong person or taken a wrong turn on the walk back to the hotel, I could have died.

We've all had run-ins with death. Whether we meet the grim reaper after a crazy night out or in a depressive slump, we all understand that that meeting won't be our last. Someday, death will come and take us with it. Anything that is living ends up dying. It's THE cycle. It's a depressing truth we don't like to think about, but it is the truth.

We are GODs, but we are not immortal.

While it might be fun to never think about dying, never attend another funeral, and never have another near-death experience, that's not the way life works. When death shows up, we all have a similar reaction to it: fight for survival at all costs.

Fighting for survival is like swimming upstream. Life would be easier if we swam downstream instead. When it comes to death, we can swim with the flow by accepting and exploring our feelings around the topic, rather than struggling to escape.

When I was 19, I was the poster child for teenage angst: lost, confused, and depressed. One evening, the thought of killing myself–of ending the confusion–crossed my mind. I wanted to go out and do something stupid, but my mom kept me at home. The feeling passed and after, I received thoughts about how to make my life my own. I decided I would be more in control of my life, not others.

Before I had those thoughts, I was drinking heavily to cope with the confusion and lostness. I'd drink one bottle of whisky a week, on top of lots of wine to numb and forget myself.

Afterward, I started acting as if I had control. I dropped out of the engineering program and joined the military. I drank less to escape and more for fun. I thought of who I would want to be with romantically, my now-wife came to mind, so I called her for a date. I wouldn't have had any of this if I had killed myself.

Staring at death made me reevaluate my life. It gave me the courage to improve my life and pursue my dreams. If we ignore death, we avoid life, as one can't exist without the other. Just by living, we risk death, but that doesn't mean we shouldn't live.

If Jan is afraid of flying, she might decide to never get on a plane. Not flying allows Jan to avoid death in a plane crash, but it also means she'll never fulfill her dream of visiting Bali.

If Jeff always sits in his room, gripped with fear of the world outside, he'll also miss out on every life experience, from making friends to eating amazing food to feeling the sun on his skin.

To reach our dreams we need to dance with death.

If we want to truly live, we also need to be aware that we can die at any time. No one knows how long they have on Earth and the only time guaranteed is the present. The present is the time to take the risks worth taking: book that plane ticket, apply for that amazing job opportunity, and tell those we care about that we love them 🩶

Many risks in life give us back experiences and opportunities that are worth it. And this is coming from someone who does risk management for their career! I always say, "ships are safe in the harbor, but that's not what they were built for."

We have to sacrifice some things that keep us safe in order to live life to the fullest. By understanding and approaching our feelings about death, we are able to fully understand the risks worth taking. Yet most of us don't see death as an opportunity to fully live–we're too busy trying to prevent it. And it makes sense. That's why our ancestors survived and procreated. But while we were built to delay death, we weren't built with proper coping mechanisms for the feelings that our eventual demise brings up.

People respond to death in a few nonsensical ways:

1. Death is the beginning of a new life.
2. Death has different meanings.
3. The closer we get to death, the wiser we are.
4. Death is a thing to avoid.

Self Discovery Exercise

WHAT ARE THE DIFFERENT RELATIONSHIPS THOSE AROUND US HAVE WITH DEATH? WHICH ONES ARE HEALTHY AND WHICH ARE UNHEALTHY?

Death is the beginning of a new life.
Most of the major religions promise an eternal life or a second life. Some people even sacrifice this life for the next one. In reality, anything that goes on for eternity would be unbearable.

In fact, one of the main traits all religions share is coming up with the promise of an afterlife. Christians, Jews, and Muslims can live eternal lives in heaven if they live a certain way. Buddhists will be reincarnated nto a form based on their karma. Hindus believe in a never-ending cycle of reincarnation. More spiritual people today believe Earth is a playground where we come for a short period to learn lessons before eturning to our true form of energy floating in space. For what we actually know, this could be hell.

Vhat the promised afterlife is doesn't matter as much as the promise that ife will continue–that this isn't the end. This not only comforts us about our own lives, but also about those who leave Earth before us. For many vho are grieving, the idea of an afterlife keeps them going, especially if heir loved one is in a better place, be it just an imaginary one.

Outside of religions, we look for signs of the afterlife. Whether it's bestselling books by those with near-death experiences, visiting a medium to get in touch with a departed loved one, or hunting for ghosts.

Vhile it's possible our energy lives on, it is not "ours" anymore. Our consciousness rides the wave of energy within our bodies for a brief ime, then disappears when we die, like a wave into the ocean. The best surfers are those we think have discovered this secret, though it could also help us outside of hanging ten.

Death has different meanings
Along with creating an afterlife, we also assign meaning to death. Often, these meanings are hierarchical and based on how it happened. Some of these definitions are meant to make us feel better while others control society. If someone dies young, it's a tragedy. If someone dies in heir sleep at an old age, it makes sense and is how they would have wanted to go. If someone is burned at the stake, they're a witch.

While that last one isn't used much today, there is a similar one which is very alive today: if someone dies fighting for their country, religion, or people, they are a hero. Those who die in battle have always been romanticized. War itself has even been romanticized. Most history classes today focus on the dates and details of wars and battles. Other historical events aren't talked about as much or if they are discussed, they are secondary to wars. Instead of studying the greatest triumphs of humans, we study the worst parts.

This interpretation is the most dangerous–it makes the masses easier to control because their deaths for a country or religion are valiant. In the ages of the Vikings and Romans, leaders fought alongside their tribes. The Vikings glorified death in battle so much, it was the only type of death that would get one into Valhalla, aka Viking heaven. But leaders today aren't trained to fight. Instead they use this valor of fighting in battle to get others to die for them.

The closer we get to death, the wiser we are
As we've discussed in previous chapters, we like to view life as one upward line, not a cycle with ups and downs. What happens when this desire for things to only get better meets with death? We overvalue the wisdom of older generations.

When we see older generations as the wise, all-knowing people amongst us because they've been on Earth longer, we give them too much power. It's why 65 year-olds who don't know how to convert a PDF to a Word Document are still in charge of major corporations and the average age of world leaders is well above 50 years old.

The closer to death, the more fearful we can get about losing what we have. This leads to some poor decisions because we're not thinking ahead to future generations. We would spend 20,000 euros to cure a person to give them two more years, but spending 20,000 euros on a healthy six-year-old would be less acceptable. In fact, most countries spend more on health and retirement for people in their last 20 years than on education and preventative health measures for people in their first 20. We are always running behind instead of running ahead.

This might be due to the fact that older people vote the most, and often they vote to maintain the status quo, even if it's not the best move for society. This skews our societies towards the needs and beliefs of older populations, even though they are the ones with the least amount of time left.

Introducing a **maximum voting age**, like we have a minimum, would help reduce this skew, as older people would be prevented from voting out of fear and spite.

One could argue who would defend the rights of the older generation if they can't vote, but today the youngest generation is not voting, and their rights are still guaranteed. They trust their parents, and in turn, their parents should trust them. The oldest dilemma in the world 😄

This isn't to say older leaders don't have a place in our communities–they do!–but we also need a larger share of younger voices in positions of influence to counterbalance older generations when they act out of fear of death (see Brexit), and not from their experience and wisdom.

Instead of constant growth, human development goes up and down. While older generations do have experience we can learn from, they are not in the prime decision-making years, have an old-fashioned mindset, and act out of fear. Because they are afraid of dying and want back what they had when they were young, they vote to maintain the status quo or even to regress things back to how life was when they were younger–**a diabolical illusion.**

Instead of overvaluing those who are the oldest, we should shift the power to the center of life. Those in the middle of their life are more likely to act out of logic over fear and to care for the young and old.

Death is a thing to avoid.
As I mentioned at the beginning of the book, most of us tend to live as if this is not the only life we have–as if this life is just a dress rehearsal. That creates an illusion over our lives: we believe we will have other chances. Other chances even beyond this finite reality. That, I am afraid, is not the case.

consider this misconception to be mostly fueled by our fear of death and our inability to come to terms with it. We struggle to admit that we are bound to this single experience and rather than accepting our individual fate, we create a series of fantasies to deal with our fear.

As a consequence, no one speaks about death. It is almost a taboo and it's seen as something we should forget about. However, this approach generates a vicious circle, as the less we speak about death, the less we are likely to come to terms with its inevitability. It is the only thing in the universe we will all experience, yet we try to ignore it. My advice is to embrace it.

What I mean by embracing it is not to be understood as striving for it. It is about ensuring that it is going to be one of the focal points of our existence. Many of us make the non-existing afterlife the focal point of their life, some others make themselves the focus, and still others decide life itself is where their attention should go.

If we were to recognize death as the end of our existence, we would then handle everything else in relation to it. This would allow us to better accept it and shape our desires around targets within the scope of this reality. **To live life is to risk death.**

WHICH RISKS ARE WORTH TAKING AND WHICH AREN'T? HOW CAN OUR GUT INSTINCTS HELP DRIVE THESE DECISIONS?

On our own, we are GODs that don't know much, that blame and suppose, and that even die. We have our shortcomings and our time on Earth is even shorter. Most people stumble through life, over half their dreams unrealized as they get distracted. Not quite the idea of god we are sold. So how exactly can we effectively generate our dreams, not chaos?

The one godlike superpower we have is love. When we love, we take ownership and we live on in other GODs, as we influespire the world surrounding us. Let's learn to use and spread this superpower in the next–and final–chapter.

Chapter 10:
Bonus Track

When we hear the word love, what comes to mind? For many people it's romantic love. Our society is inundated with movies, books, and messages that romantic love is the answer to all our problems. The plotline of almost every romantic comedy is that some woman's life is riddled with problems; as she falls in love with that annoying coworker or handyman from a small town, she realizes that what was missing all along was romantic love. A magic wand transforms her life into perfection as she kisses the main love interest at the end.

Romance can narrow what we believe love can be. But if we focus too much on romantic love, we close ourselves off to the many other forms it can take. We can give and receive love from friends, family, children, pets, jobs, sports, hobbies, and even strangers.

If we expand that definition to include more types of love, our lives will become fuller. Only craving one type of love robs us of the love which is all around—when we broaden our focus, **we can be rich in love!**

Love is truly all we need–even if it's cliche (some cliches are that way because they are true!). But this love needs to extend into all our actions, not just our romantic lives. To help illustrate how we can act out of love, I have a drinking story... where I don't drink. Basically, it's an anti-drinking story which is just as embarrassing as the drinking stories in all the previous chapters.

One Sunday, my wife and kids went to Leiden while I had to go to a three day conference at a hotel in Amsterdam. Before the conference started, I had a morning alone–a truly glorious gift for a parent–and a massage booked at the hotel. That morning, I went for my normal weekend run. Usually, I run about 10K in order to spend more time with my children, but the solitude allowed me to run for longer. The goal was to do at least 20 km, 30 km max.

But I made a mistake any seasoned runner, including myself, would be ashamed of. I wore too many layers and quickly, the heat settled into my body. My long sleeved shirt trapped the warmth, causing me to sweat and get thirsty earlier.

Luckily, I found a water fountain at the 15th kilometer, so I could freshen up a bit, but after that, there was no water to be seen. At around 25 kilometers, I stopped and walked the last three home. Walking three kilometers took longer than running it, especially when every bone in my body was screaming out for water.

As I approached my house, my body sank in relief. Finally, a chance to rest and drink some water. But when I saw the time on the clock, every muscle tensed up again and a new wave of exhaustion hit. I had to be on the 2:49pm train to get to my massage... and I got home from my run/walk around 1:40.

I made two sandwiches as fast as possible. Not only were those sandwiches saltier and drier than usual, I paired them with coke instead of water. I then showered and threw whatever clothes I could find into my suitcase. In less than 60 minutes, I was out the door, panting as if I'd just finished my run a minute earlier. The train was nine minutes away and the station was a 13 minute walk, so I decided to bike... with my suitcase. Only in Amsterdam, am I right?

The bike wobbled this way and that as the suitcase shifted. If it wasn't hard enough to bike with a suitcase, one wheel came off my suitcase halfway there. With three wheels, I looked like a clown wobbling on a unicycle, trying anything to stay afloat. At the station, I locked my bike and ran through the train doors a moment before they closed. I slammed down in a seat, breathing so hard even the conductor could hear me.

As I took out my phone, an email from the hotel popped up. Through exhaustion, I struggled to make out what the message said: ...regret to inform... cancellation... relaxing massage...

No way! All that effort, pain, and stress had been for nothing. When I called the front desk, they first tried to say I hadn't checked in on time–but it was almost 3pm and my check-in was three. Then they said the masseuse called in sick. I pointed out that the reasoning changed during the call, frustration growing inside me.

As I got off the phone, we were leaving Amstel station and the train spun. I sweated more as my breathing grew ragged. There wasn't a reason to rush anymore. My mind had lost control of my body–a body which was in full on panic mode.

As the train slowed to the next stop, I got up. Others leaving at the same stop gave me a wide berth, some looking concerned, others frustrated by my lack of control. Their reactions didn't matter though. All that mattered was getting some fresh air and finding a way to calm down. I walked straight out, let go of the suitcase halfway down the platform, and looked for oncoming trains. No trains came from the other side, so I walked over to the tracks and threw up.

For the first time in my life, I was throwing up not because of too many liquids, but because of too few liquids.

And unlike when I threw up from drinking too much, everything I threw up this time was dry. There was no liquid, just pieces of sandwich that I had to force out of my throat so I wouldn't choke. Luckily, I was at the far end of the station and didn't mentally scar anyone but myself.

Once I vomited everything in my stomach, I sat down on the station's steps, more winded than I had been right aft er my run. I was done.

(In)sane Drinking Wisdom
ALWAYS DRINK ENOUGH WATER.
IT'S SUCH A SIMPLE**, BUT IMPACTFUL ADVICE.**
HYDRATE 💧 OR DIEDRATE ⚰️

A couple of trains came and went, taking with them anyone who might have seen me throw up earlier. The trains also brought newcomers and there were more people on the platform. People stepped around me, but never stopped and asked how I was doing–and anyone with two eyes could see I needed help!

At that point, I could still muster up the energy to leave the train station. Just get out, call an uber to the hotel, and everything will be ok, I repeated to myself. With each step, the idea became more fragmented and my thoughts blurred.

The sweltering summer heat greeted me like an annoying coworker as I emerged from the train station. After a few moments in the sun, exhaustion had won the battle. I collapsed, half laying on my elbow, in the sun, on the corner of the sidewalk.

Pedestrians, bikes, and cars whirled by, but no one stopped to ask if I was ok. Some people would give me wary looks or intentionally walk around me, with very little compassion in their eyes. At least a hundred people passed, but no one would stop.

"Is everything ok?" a voice finally said.

I blinked up, making out the figure standing between the sun and me. The man stared back at me, concern plastered on his face. This man was nothing more than skin and bones. He had to be in his late 40s, judging from the wrinkles and smile lines forming on his face, and he spoke with a heavy Arab accent. He pushed back a piece of his graying hair as he set his 15 euros bike aside and crouched next to me.

I gave him a smile as he sat and he grinned back, revealing missing teeth. The ones he still had were yellowed and crooked, the obvious wear of life eating away. The man wore an old Bayern Munich Adidas tracksuit, but what really caught my attention about his clothing were the swimming pool slippers he wore with white socks.

"Water," I croaked as a way of answering his question. The idea of water was refreshing, but I wondered where this guy was going to go to find it and how long it would take. Within a minute, he came back with a cup of water and helped me move into the shade across the street.

"Bring the cup back to that building when done," the man said, pointing to a building nearby. He went over to his bike and fished around in two grocery bags hanging off the beaten-up handles. Finally, he pulled out a plum. "That will help too," he said as he rode off on his bike.

ate the plum, bit by tiny bit, to go easy on the stomach. I felt better after, but decided to rest. After two short naps, I gathered my strength and walked over to bring the cup back. When I entered the building the man pointed to, it was a local mosque. The building had been so uniform, so like the office buildings surrounding it, that I hadn't expected to find a place of worship. There were a couple of people talking inside, so I crept in, left the cup next to the sink, and left.

After that, I called an uber and went to the hotel. On the uber ride, and many times after, I thought of that man. If I had seen someone like me had been in trouble, I would have stopped to help without a second thought. But if the person in difficulty had been someone from another status, like the man who helped me, I might not have stopped before that day.

The realization made me reexamine my life and how I sometimes acted out of fear, not love. I would have stopped and helped someone who looked like me (aka someone from an in-group) because I wasn't afraid of them, but I wouldn't have helped someone from another culture or someone who looked homeless because I feared it might have been a trick. And that was an issue that I needed to address.

That day reminded me to act out of love more often than fear. But what exactly does this look like? Before we can learn how to act, we need to first define the two states we can choose to live in: fear and love.

FEAR: False Evidence Appearing Real
Much of the modern world presents us with false evidence that we and the people around us should be in competition, not communion. In fact, the entire economic system many of us live and work in is based on a couple of fear principles, including the prisoner's dilemma.

The prisoner's dilemma is a thought experiment to determine how most individuals will act if presented with two options; one benefits them while the other benefits the entire group, but costs them.

Let's say there are two prisoners: Noel and Liam. They are both arrested for robbing a convenience store, but the evidence is weak, with only a grainy security camera catching the act. The officer needs a confession to convict them and brings in Noel first. He tells him, "Confess that Liam robbed the bank and he will serve five years." In this case, Noel would be free to go.

Next, he brings in Liam and says the same thing. Testify against Noel, and Liam is free and Noel gets five years.

But if they both testify against each other, they will both get three years in prison. If they both remain silent, each gets one year.

Since the two can't cooperate, they will testify against each other as it is the strategy that guarantees the best outcome for each individual without knowing what the other one is doing. In this situation, the lack of knowledge and cooperation creates false evidence that betraying their friend is the best overall strategy for them. In reality, it is not.

When we're divided, as in-groups and out-groups, we will default to the lose/lose situation instead of the win/win because we fear that others might get more than us. That's why division, often under the guise of promoting individualism, is a main attribute of consumerist cultures. When we're divided, we're more likely to be in a scarcity mindset, always afraid the resources will dry up for us or we won't be able to find another job. Out of this fear, we hoard. We consume more, harming the Earth, and hold on tight to any opportunities we get, afraid others will take them away from us or that we'll never find something better.

All of these actions are based on fear and scarcity instead of cooperation and compassion for others. This approach is based on the belief that we don't love each other and everyone is out to win for themselves, not to win for everyone. When we think we are alone in this world, we are at our weakest.

To love = to care.

The beauty of the prisoner's dilemma is that it also shows us that when we cooperate, we get the best result for everyone involved. Liam and Noel would have both gotten just one year if they had been allowed to communicate.

But there is another solution that does not require communication: they trusted and loved each other to the point of knowing that the other one would never betray them. In a world of love, where we care for those around us, there are abundant possibilities for everyone.

Instead of fighting over resources and opportunities, we come together because we care about others, and through our dreams create even more opportunities. In this utopian world, Liam and Noel would not have even tried to rob the bank.

Of course, this is a dream world, but we are GODs and we can work toward it by building strong communities within our families, groups of friends or a workplace. When we love someone or something, we process our surroundings and act from that love in three steps:

- **Step 1**: I establish if I love something and then determine how much I care about it. This realization can happen naturally or I could sit down and reflect on what truly matters to me.
- **Step 2**: Once I figure out what I care about I pursue that thing with ease. If we take extreme actions or hold on tightly to what we want, we are actually acting out of fear. We believe the false evidence that the person, experience, or thing we love can be taken from us.
- **Step 3**: Calmly push through any doubt and struggles. One of the biggest lies society tells us is that "if one loves what they do, they'll never work a day in their life." This sort of lie isn't just in our professional lives, but in every area. So often, we're told that true love is easy–it's riding off into the sunset or finding that friend we never argue with. But the reality is the things, experiences, and people we love are often the ones that challenge us the most.

Before we put it all together and determine how love can rule our lives, let's dive into the three main steps further, as they can be confusing.

What do we care about?

The first step toward living from love is to determine what exactly we love. As we've discussed, we're so often limited in our definition of love. Some of us think it only applies to romantic partners, while others think it only applies to romantic partners, family, and friends.

But when we have such a narrow, individualistic definition of love, we deprive ourselves of more joy. More love and compassion are never dangerous. It's possible to extend that love and have empathy for everyone around us, the Earth, and everything on it. When we consciously care about everyone we meet we make the world–and our lives–a better place.

The man who saved me from dehydration is a good example of that and I'm sure he does many other small things, other than saving me, which make his community and our world better.

Act from ease, not desperation

While our definition of love is positive, not everyone has a positive conception of love. Too often, it can turn into obsession, violence, and control. But when we abuse or try to control the people and situations we love, it's no longer love. At this point, it has shifted into the fear of losing the object of our adoration. And let's keep in mind that this is a VERY thin line.

Obviously, few people would hurt their loved ones consciously, but subconsciously, it's all too easy to slip into this fear mindset and hold on too tightly.

One of the best examples of this is helicopter parents. Like most parents, these folks love their children. Unlike other parents, they are constantly hovering around their children, trying to make sure no harm comes to them. They're holding on too tightly to their relationship with their child, which stifles the child's free will and doesn't set them up for success and living an autonomous life. It can also make the child resentful, bringing about the result the parents wanted least: less love between them and their child.

This can also be true of dreams, experiences, and things as well as people. For example, a sports fan can desperately want his team to win the World Cup. He says he will kill for his team... and after his team loses, he's angry enough to harm others. Sadly, so are others who invested too deeply in the same team, so they riot together in the streets.

We can also harm ourselves instead of others–especially when we hold on to an idea of how something is supposed to be instead of letting life unfold. Let's say we dream of being a writer, and we start writing a bit every day. We are convinced we can make it without any help, and we continue down this path for years writing, but without ever becoming a writer. In a way, we fail to see that we are choking on our own dreams.

If we truly love our dream, we need to approach it with ease. This would allow us to see that attempting to make it without help is not working and makes us reconsider our strategy earlier. We might then decide to take writing lessons, thus taking a step closer to the realization of our dream. By moving into our dream with ease, the dream will love us back.

When we hold on too tight or try too hard, the things we love slip away. GODs should hold on to dreams lightly. They should feel lightly, move lightly, and react lightly. As GODs, we have a chance every day to let go, to move lighter, and to place more emphasis on feeling good than the outcome itself. We can choose to focus on lighter emotions instead of sinking into pity and fear.

Growing from the struggles

While we shouldn't hold on too tightly to the things we love, it doesn't mean we won't have to struggle for them. There's a difference between easing our way into love and not addressing any problems in our relationships with others, our careers, or our communities. Acting lightly is different than taking no loving actions at all, just because we are afraid of trying too hard or holding on too tightly. As I mentioned before, the line is VERY, VERY, VERY thin.

Often it's the people, dreams, and experiences we love that challenge us the most. When a challenge does arise, we have two options: to run away and lose what we love or stay and fight. With the second option, we most likely will learn something new about ourselves and deepen our love for that person, dream, or experience.

Let's say there's a married couple who love each other very much, but recently they've been fighting more often than usual. The "easy" option would be to sink into fear and give up. But that's not committing to their love for one another. To commit, they would need to work through the argument and come out stronger on the other side. But for it to work, **it must be a joint dream and effort**, not one-sided.

The same could be said when pursuing a dream. While someone can work toward their dream of being a writer with ease, it doesn't mean they won't face struggles. When an obstacle appears, they can sink back, never realizing their dream, or they can face it head-on and see what happens.

When we work through the struggles, we can take our places as GODs in any area of our lives!

Self Discovery Exercise
IN WHAT WAYS DO WE ACT
OUT OF LOVE AND OUT OF FEAR?
WHAT ARE SOME OTHER EXAMPLES THAN THE
SITUATIONS ABOVE?

By approaching each decision from a place of love, not fear, one's perception of the world can change.

For example, let's say Marco is walking down the street and he sees someone walking the other way. If he acted out of fear, Marco would glance down, afraid to make eye contact because this stranger could hurt him.

f he acted out of love, Marco would smile. The stranger, seeing a friendly face, could take the opportunity to ask him if he is right for the station and find out that he is not. But Marco is actually going there himself and can walk with him.

Fast forward two years and Marco and the stranger could be best friends. Or maybe the two smile at each other and head their separate ways, both feeling a little warmer at the kindness the other showed.

Each minute, we can vote with our actions for which world we want to live in. Do we want to open our world up to new people, opportunities, and experiences? Or do we want to cower back to what we already know?

In the central nine chapters of this book, we discussed the different influespire levels of our lives and some fundamental areas for each one of them:

- The societal (religion, patriotism, and racism)
- The pack (work, friends, and family)
- The individual (knowledge, ownership, and death)

In every area, people choose fear too often and don't choose love enough. We act from fear as a society when we force our nationalistic beliefs and religious ideologies onto others or categorize based on skin color or any other form of difference. Fear infects our packs when we stay in jobs, friendships, and family situations we dislike, scared that we'll never find anything better. And of course, many individuals act out of fear, whether that's the fear of learning new things or not knowing enough, not wanting to take ownership of their mistakes, or simply being afraid of dying.

But what if we reanalyzed these areas and saw how we could better deal with negativity and the downward cycles? We could create something more fulfilling, something made of love. Imagine where we would be today had we started the shift away from fear toward love earlier.

If we choose love now, it might not solve every instance of racism, every conflict between nations, and each disagreement between religions. It might not even help our family members or make toxic friendships healthier. But it will make us as individuals a bit happier and possibly cause a ripple effect that could impact us all. The desert moves one grain of sand at a time.

We can choose to love life instead of fear death, to take chances for what we care about, and to pursue our love of knowledge. Those individual pursuits can better humanity via big actions, like devoting our career to a social cause, and small actions, such as smiling at a stranger on the street.

Acting from love might not fix all the problems on Earth in an instant, but it's a place to start. It's the only place to start. And love is who we've been all along.

We would have never been able to make it this far if we did not care for each other. Humanity evolved through millennia by loving each other, despite fearing each other. And that love is ingrained in our DNA—it's the key to living fuller lives and building stronger, better communities and societies.

We are GODs of love ♥

Printed in Poland
by Amazon Fulfillment
Poland Sp. z o.o., Wrocław

20774581R00107